ROBERT COOVER'S FICTIONS

ROBERT COOVER'S FICTIONS

Jackson I. Cope

THE JOHNS HOPKINS UNIVERSITY PRESS

Baltimore and London

The Johns Hopkins University Press
701 West 40th Street
Baltimore, Maryland 21211
The Johns Hopkins Press Ltd., London

The paper used in this publication meets the minimum requirements of
American National Standard for Information Sciences — Permanence of
Paper for Printed Library Materials, ANSI Z39.48-1984.

Library of Congress Cataloging-in-Publication Data

Cope, Jackson I.
   Robert Coover's fictions.

   Includes index.
   1. Coover, Robert — Criticism and interpretation. I. Title.
PS3553.0633Z65 1986   813'.54   86-45445
ISBN 0-8018-3365-5 (alk. paper)

Citation rights for the following works by Robert Coover have been
generously granted: *The Universal Baseball Association, Inc., J. Henry
Waugh, Prop.,* Copyright © 1968 by Robert Coover. Reprinted by per-
mission of the publisher, Random House, Inc.; *Pricksongs & Descants,*
Copyright © 1969 by Robert Coover. Reprinted by permission of the
publisher, E. P. Dutton, a division of New American Library; "Whatever
Happened to Gloomy Gus of the Chicago Bears?" Copyright © 1975 by
Robert Coover. Reprinted by permission of the publisher, *American
Review,* Bantam Books, Inc.; *The Public Burning,* Copyright © 1976,
1977 by Robert Coover. Reprinted by permission of the publisher, The
Viking Press; *Spanking the Maid,* Copyright © 1982 by Robert Coover.
Reprinted by permission of the publisher, Grove Press, Inc.; "You Must
Remember This," Copyright © 1984 by *Playboy.* Reprinted by permis-
sion of the publisher, *Playboy; Gerald's Party,* Copyright © 1985 by
Robert Coover. Reprinted by permission of the publisher, Linden Press,
a division of Simon & Schuster, Inc. *A Night at the Movies: You Must
Remember This,* Copyright © by Robert Coover, forthcoming in 1987
from Linden Press, a division of Simon & Schuster, Inc.

For DeAnn,
un ricordo di Venezia ed amore

CONTENTS

PREFACE

The following pages are neither authorized nor impersonal. I encountered Coover's baseball novel serendipitously while scanning the incredibly crowded and miscellaneous shelves of a sublet summer apartment in Montreal in 1969. At least, I had thought it was a baseball novel until I read the first two pages. I had to read on through a good deal of contemporary fiction and theory of fiction to understand its context and its author's uniqueness. It was a pleasure, and an education that is implicit rather than recited in this book.

By good fortune, I came to know Robert Coover as a friend some time after that first encounter with Coover as author. When I invented the idea of this work, of writing upon that invention, some years ago, we agreed that I would treat it as I had perforce treated the canons of other victims of my critical pleasures – Glanvill, Joyce, Milton – without privileged information. The agreement has been largely honored. Coover has permitted me to read and cite "Aesop's Forest" and the extended version of "Gloomy Gus" from yet unpublished manuscripts. Aside from an old essay on *The Universal Baseball Association, Inc. (Iowa Review* 2, no. 4 [1971]), to whose editors I am indebted, Coover has read none of the words, judgments, interpretations that follow. I only guess that curiosity has led him through that early attempt.

In writing about Coover, I hope and suspect that I am writing about the possibilities, the closures and reopenings, inherent in the novel. That, after all, is the genre toward which we have moved in a faith of perfectibility for something like three hundred years. And we begin to learn about a great writer by beginning with the genre in which he writes. We learn the values and shape of that genre by watching attentively what he does to alter them. What I offer is a reading in some of Robert Coover's fictions into which is incorporated a rivulet that essays the importance of the forms of modern fiction.

What is not presented here is a survey of Coover's work; that has been made elsewhere, if not wisely nor too well. Neither will one find comparisons, placings of a writer among his contemporaries. That, too, is plentifully available to those who find it useful (the most coherent achievement is a surprisingly compressed essay that I would recommend to one seeking a primer or a placing for Coover's work: Kathryn Hume, "Robert Coover's Fiction: The Naked and the Mythic," *Novel* 12 [1979]: 127–48).

If I speak of "modern" fiction, it is to remind us that we are past "postmodernism." The burning issues in criticism of the past two decades have burned out in the best way: They flared alarmingly, burned down into a hard core of truth haloed by blue flame from the devil's disciples, and gave Coover and other serious fictionalists of his generation a generic photograph of themselves against which to react in a re-creative way. All that theorizing was a good thing, but it has been reabsorbed into the novel, and novelists, fiction writers, are getting on with the job. I offer some readings in how one of them is doing.

I am indebted to the John Simon Guggenheim Foundation for a fellowship that made it possible to spend much of a year in Venice studying Venetian drama. I stole a couple of those months of indulgence to complete this reading, which seemed suddenly necessary of harvest.

Jane Warth was patient and penetrating in trying to make my mind and my prose parse. Leslie Fiedler read it all with generosity. Pili Coover added to its elegance, as she has done to my life.

Eric Halpern did more than anyone toward the fruition of this book, for which a simple thanks.

ABBREVIATIONS

Abbreviated references in the text are to the following:

UBA   Robert Coover, *The Universal Baseball Association, Inc., J. Henry Waugh, Prop.* (New York: Random House, 1968).

P&D   ———, *Pricksongs & Descants: Fictions* (New York: Dutton, 1969).

PB   ———, *The Public Burning* (New York: Viking, 1977).

SM   ———, *Spanking the Maid* (New York: Grove, 1982).

GP   ———, *Gerald's Party* (New York: Simon and Schuster, 1986).

ANM   ———, *A Night at the Movies: You Must Remember This* (New York: Simon and Schuster, forthcoming in 1987).

First Person   ———, Interview in *First Person: Conversations on Writers and Writing*, ed. Frank Gado (Schenectady, N.Y.: Union College Press, 1983), 142–59.

Dostoevsky   Mikhail Bakhtin, *Problems of Dostoevsky's Poetics*, ed. and trans. Caryl Emerson (Minneapolis: University of Minnesota Press, 1984).

Dialogic   ———, *The Dialogic Imagination: Four Essays*, ed. Michael Holquist, trans. Caryl Emerson and Michael Holquist (Austin: University of Texas Press, 1981).

xi

ROBERT COOVER'S FICTIONS

PROLOGUE

"At first," once upon no time, "in an instant half-real half-remembered, the leper is at rest; then he begins his approach." The landscape is mythic, perhaps allegorical: the "sun at its zenith . . . dazzling white this figure crossing the molten red flats, his outline blurred by the savage glare" (*P&D*, 179). A medieval *Totentanz*, "he merely dances on, arms and legs outflung, . . . scratching his helix across the desert floor, . . . his steaming white helix on the burnt red plane. His robe seems not so much a robe as a . . . winding sheet! *Death!*" (180). But, no, the echo is complicated and crossed by the incursions of other echoes that are also to be denied priority. The leper moves in a crazy helix because the narrator, "we," moves us in a "precise, governed" pattern "so regulating our own velocity as to schedule his [the leper's] arrival . . . at our starting point" (180). It is a game, a hunt in which the leper is only an object on the geometrical psyche of the hunted narrator. But as the physical distance closes ("Down the last arc segment we glide, closing it now . . . he is close enough now for us to see his eager smile" [181]) the narrator's cool voice becomes less objectively distanced, nervously observant of detail that he tries to dismiss: "tattered ends of his white flesh confusing themselves with . . . his fluttering robe, flake off a scaly dust . . . translucent layers of dead scaly material, here and there hardened into shiny nodules, here and there disturbed by deep cavities. In the beds of these cavities: a dark substance, resembling blood not so much as . . . as: excrement. Well, simple illusion, blood mixed with pus and baked in the sun, that's what it is" (181). And then the voice becomes hysterical, the voice of Faustus and Everyman: "But now — oh my god! — as a mere few paces separate us, our point of origin — and end! — just visible before us, the brute reality

1

slams through the barriers of our senses: 'the encounter is now imminent!'" (181). "The leper, tongue dangling . . . whole wretched body
oozing a kind of milky sweat, hurls himself into our arms, smother-
ing us, pitching us to the red clay, his sticky cold flesh fastening to
us, me, his black tongue licking my face" (182). One recalls the folk
terror, the frequent legends of curse from the leper's kiss. And yet,
the narrator seems to seek his destiny even after he has recognized its
inevitability and its horror: "Our hands, 'my' hand, appear before
us . . . extended now for the embrace" (181); "I lie helpless under the
sickening weight of his perishing flesh. Then, in the same instant, it is
over. Purged of all revulsions . . . we lay him gently on the red
earth, dry his final ecstatic tears" (182). The objectivity and the horror have both been displaced by an unexpected loosing of resignation, charity, recognition, and acceptance, Saint Francis turning
back to give the leper a kiss, or Edward the Confessor bearing the
leper upon his back. And we are within that other tradition of the
leper, that of Saint Julien L'Hospitalier, Flaubert's oedipal hunter.
The hunter hunted: the noble youth with a blood lust upon whom
the great black stag, last of the slaughtered, impresses the curse of
parricide; fleeing this curse he fulfills it; doing penance he is himself
hunted down by the hideous leper for whom no service is sufficient,
no embrace close enough until Julien has given his entire body and
the pariah Christ calls Julien to salvation. But if Flaubert's saint and
divine leper seem imposed upon the dance of death, upon the leper's
curse in a legendary palimpsest, the last phrases of the narrator invert the relationships, invert the assumptions we have had about the
pronoun "we" he has used throughout, and seem to fuse him now
with the leper rather than ourselves, to force us into his own position
by suddenly separating us from it: "We leave him lie and sit beside to
wait. Under the desert sun. We wait, as he waited for us, for you.
Desperate in need, yet with terror. What terrible game will 'you' play
with 'us'? me" (182).

The leper writhing and the desert setting under the noonday sun
(that detail itself sufficient to activate a tradition of demons and
temptation, one returns to this in reading *The Public Burning*) offer
us an allegorical figure in an allegorical landscape. Yet they do not
sustain themselves in spite of their richness. The leper is neither
Christ nor curse nor defined; the desert is not a place of isolation,

dessication, but that place where leper and narrator are united in an apparent covenant of self-recognition. And where we shall come to them. In the end, each man is Death, each the leper, in that he chooses death: "Had we thought, only thought, we could have drawn two circles, or ten circles, postponed this ultimate experience, could have, but the choice was ours just once, our impulsive first action has become — alas! — a given, the inexorable governor of all that remains." Or is this the illusion: "Has the leper had us all along? did his pace allow two circles? and does it matter?" (181). No, the choice is all one, like the agent of that choice, as the narrator makes clear when he embraces the leper, replaces the leper, to await our replacement in and through him. The narrative "we" is only an apparent shift from one polarity of alliance with the narrator to the other: "We" are three persons in one.

What has happened to the palimpsest of sources, the aborted allegories is that the internal structure of the story has raised its several layers to the light, then absorbed them into a reinterpretation. But the reinterpretation is not that of myths modernized; beginning to sense how it could be created, Coover does not emulate the syncretism of *Finnegans Wake*, but mocks it. The internal structure of "The Leper's Helix," it will have become apparent, is movement, movement plotted by the rules of a solid geometry upon a surface that is ephemeral time and space: "He has always been beginning, always approaching, it was the glare, just the glare caused the illusion" (179). This movement itself replaces and becomes the allegory of the union of life and death through choice, the dance of death given a new dimension of psychic rather than externalized necessity.

But the geometric movement itself, once recognized as allegory, invokes another analogue that allows us to think of the problem in a new dimension again, as that irrationality of rationality, the self-invalidation of orders, yet the inevitability of pattern.

"The Leper's Helix" appears in *Pricksongs & Descants*, which Coover labels "Fictions," and "ficciones" is a word appropriated to cover his particular mode of cerebral imagining by Jorge Luis Borges. The impact of Borges upon Coover has probably been of major importance: They share an unremitting interest in the loss of self through the act of imaginative projection, and in the attempts to reconstruct (perhaps to recover) that self in the teasingly predictable forms of number and measure. Let us set the inner and outer, spatial and temporal geometry of "The Leper's Helix" against that of Borges' "Death and the Compass" ("La Muerte y la brujula").[1]

Written in appropriately melodramatic style, it is a detective story (as is Coover's later novel *Gerald's Party*). The first murder victim is a delegate to a Talmudic Congress who has written a shelf of books on Jewish mysticism, hermetic numerology, and names. The detective Lönnrot, noting the statement "the first letter of the Name has been uttered" on a scrap at the scene of the crime, takes away the victim's hermetic writings to study for a solution. A second and third crime occur at intervals of just one month; at each scene, in some form, harlequin costumes, paint swathes, diamonds of color ("yellow, red and green diamonds") appear. The second letter is uttered, then the "last" letter. As though to confirm the close of sequence, the police receive a map of the city marking the points of the three murders as precisely equidistant, forming "the perfect vertices of a mystic equilateral triangle." The hermetic sacrificial murders have been completed. But Lönnrot remembers the inevitable diamonds at each crime, knows that the Tetragrammaton is made up of four letters, JHVH (Jehovah, Yawah), and so refuses to be thrown off, seeking out the equidistant fourth point that will complete the diamond, seeking it on the fourth day of the fourth month, and finding it at the deserted villa Triste-le-Roy. As he travels toward the lonely tryst with death, he smiles at the thought that his archenemy, the vengeance-seeking gunman Red Scharlach, would give a great deal to know he was in such an exposed spot; then "Lönnrot considered the remote possibility that the fourth victim might be Scharlach himself. Then he rejected the idea . . . mere circumstance, reality, names . . . hardly interested him now." But names interest the reader a great deal, here reminded that the Teutonic surnames both mean *red*, that detective and criminal, hunter and hunted, here, as in "The Leper's Helix," are doubles, merged and opposed selves.

Finding the villa, Lönnrot circles it, returns to his starting point, pushes open the gate, and finds the house "abounded in pointless symmetries and in maniacal repetitions . . . one balcony was reflected in another balcony; double stairways led to double balustrades. A two-faced Hermes projected a monstrous shadow . . . . He

1. *Labyrinths*, ed. Donald A. Yates and James E. Ioby (New York, 1964), 76–87.

4

ascended . . . to circular antechambers . . . By way of a spiral staircase he arrived at the oriel. The early evening moon shone through the diamonds of the window; they were yellow, red and green. An astonishing, dizzying recollection struck him." At the moment of realization he is seized by Scharlach's men. The terms of his equation reverse: The last point of the mystic square, which will reveal the secret names, becomes the original point (even as Coover's narrator has scheduled the leper's arrival "at our starting point").

Scharlach explains that the villa was where he lay in agonized hiding with a gunshot wound suffered in a raid led by Lönnrot; he lay swearing vengeance "nine days and nine nights" — a mystic number that might remind us that Satan and his metamorphosed angels fell "nine times the space that measures day and night," that might remind us that Lönnrot is always seen in those nebulous dividing points, dawn and twilight. But a number, too, that reminds us that the three murders were reported as occurring on the third day of each month, but really occurred on the fourth, as Lönnrot learns when he reads: "Dies Judacorum incipit ad solis occasu usque ad solis occasum diei sequentis." "'This means,' he added, 'The Hebrew day begins at sundown and lasts until the following sundown.'" This number may remind us, too, that the closed triangle was a false solution, which awaited the fulfillment of the fourth point. The numbers equivocate; the paradoxically rational symmetries that the detective has built (paradoxical because built upon mystic symbols) tumble upon impact with what he had scorned as "mere circumstances, reality." The first murder was an accident, the wrong man killed in a robbery. When Scharlach learned that Lönnrot was attempting to solve the crime by studying the victim's Hebraic books, he purchased *History of the Hasidic Sect* and learned the mysteries that he projected into the second and third murders with the knowledge that Lönnrot would discern the necessity of a symmetry built upon patterns of quadruplicity rather than triplicity and so arrive where Scharlach awaited him: "at our starting point." Irrationality, accident are plotted into a mocking paradigm of death; the apparent last point of the "perfect rhomb" is discovered to be in reality the starting point. Or is this so? Do not the points exchange position once more to lift a corner of the veil which might conceal a yet more complex order to the events? If the meaningful triples can prove to have been used with duplicity, cannot the quadruplicity itself carry a double message? If the first murder in the Hotel du Nord (Hotel du Nord, Triste-le-Roy: always these symbolic names, so teasing and indefinite) was a mistake made not even by Scharlach but a lackey in a jewel robbery, why did it occur precisely upon a north-south line with the villa where Scharlach had lain three years before? If there was no real order but that of Lönnrot's obsession with a complex rational hypothesis, what is the strange portent in the observation that Lönnrot's search for the name of the murderer in the names of God led "one of those enterprising shopkeepers who have discovered that any given man is resigned to buying any given book" to publish the history of Hasidism from which Scharlach devised his scheme of murder? If Scharlach and Lönnrot are doubles by name, if they exchange roles at that daemonic point of completion of the Tetragrammaton, perhaps their name is one of the names of God,[2] each Alpha and Omega, another strange trinity whose movements, like those of the leper, narrator, and reader in Coover's fiction, allegorizes and enacts the interplay in which life and death are united, without desire, with horror, but by choice:

"Scharlach [said Lönnrot]. When in some other incarnation you hunt me, pretent to commit (or do commit) a crime at A, then a second crime at B, eight kilometers from A, then a third crime at C, four kilometers from A and B . . . Wait for me afterwards at D, two kilometers from A and C. Again halfway from both, kill me at D, as you are now going to kill me at Triste-le-Roy."

"The next time I kill you," replied Scharlach, "I promise you that labyrinth, consisting of a single line which is invisible and unceasing."

"Invisible" because like all geometry it is psychic; "unceasing" because like all psyches it is eternal by self-definition. At D the red twins will meet at the penultimate point of return to A, the "starting point," in a version of that Zenonian paradox of the endless hunt, race, game, that so fascinates Borges, that so movingly images an eternal unfulfillment,[3] point A, Alpha, without Omega, just D, death, another beginning.

One can make two observations. In adapting Borges' influence

---

2. Captured, Lönnrot asks: "'Scharlach, are you looking for the Secret Name?' . . . Lönnrot noted in his voice a fatigued triumph, a hatred the size of the universe, a sadness not less than that hatred. 'No,' said Scharlach. 'I am seeking something more ephemeral and perishable. I am seeking Eric Lönnrot.'"

3. "Avatars of the Tortoise," in *Labyrinths*, 202–8.

(acknowledged implicitly in the generic label "fictions"), Coover does not imitate it directly, but absorbs its allegorical method, as he absorbs all of his sources, starting points, into a refiguration that permits the layers to show through just sufficiently to justify the description "palimpsest" for the relationship. Further, both of the brief fictions that I have described reveal three overlapping senses of the form of experience which persistently ("The Leper's Helix" is one of the earliest works) shape Robert Coover's otherwise varied canon. These forms are game, number (in the sense suggested by the Valéryan epigraph to *Pricksongs & Descants*: "They therefore set me this problem of the equality of appearance and numbers"), and perpetual, repetitive rituals that both destroy and define the self.

We gain some sense of the appropriateness of these three metaphors of experience when we turn to the explicit aesthetic comments Coover makes in the dedicatory "prólogo" to *Pricksongs & Descants* (76–79). Cervantes "struggles against the unconscious mythic residue in human life," against "exhausted art forms," and brings forth the novel. The exhausted art form was the Romance, which focused on "Eternal Value and Beauty," whereas the novel turned to character, to exemplary histories of men. But Cervantes' society was opening out to discover man: "It could no longer be described by magic numbers or be contained in a compact and marvelous design." Now, Coover finds that we also "seem to be standing at the end of one age and on the threshold of another." Ours, however, is the opposite of Cervantes' new age; a return, rather, into that mystic night from which Cervantes was emerging: "We seem to have moved from an open-ended, anthropocentric, humanistic, naturalistic, even — to the extent that man may be thought of as making his own universe — optimistic starting point, to one that is closed, cosmic, eternal, supernatural (in its soberest sense), and pessimistic." Cervantes' revolution in the focus of fiction "governs us — not unlike the way you found yourself abused by the conventions of the Romance." But if our world has changed, the artist in the spirit of Cervantes must reject the authority of his revolution: He must use "familiar mythic or historical forms to combat the content of those forms, and to conduct the reader . . . to the real, away from mystification to clarification, away from magic to maturity, away from mystery to revelation." Or, as "don Roberto S." puts it, fiction "must provide us with an imaginative experience which is necessary to our imaginative well-being." Don Roberto S. is Robert Scholes, a colleague of Coover's at the University of Iowa, and later at Brown. The statement is from Scholes' *The Fabulators*, a study of contemporary fiction which reinforces and helps to clarify Coover's own aims. In the opening chapter, "The Revival of Romance," from which Coover is quoting, Scholes comments, apropos of Lawrence Durrell, that

> the tradition he finds thin and constricting is the very one started by Cervantes — the tradition which begins as anti-romance and gradually insists on more and more scientific treatment of life . . . Zola tried to answer the question, "What good is fiction as science?" and worked himself into the absurd corner of the "experimental" novel, a notion he seems to have had the good sense not to believe but merely to use as journalistic puffery for his own productions much as his heirs are now crying "phenomenological" novel for similar reasons.[4]

If our world has changed, our fiction must, and Scholes' casual comment on the old-fashioned quality of phenomenological fiction should be coupled with his distinction of "fabulators" as a useful gloss upon Coover's description of his own techniques and the vision they are designed to reveal. Fabulation "reveals an extraordinary delight in design. With its wheels within, wheels, rhythms and counterpoints, . . . modern fabulation, like the ancient fabling of Aesop, tends away from the representation of reality but returns toward actual human life by way of ethically controlled fantasy."[5] "The return to Being," says Coover, "has returned us to Design, to microcosmic images of the macrocosm, to the creation of Beauty within the confines of cosmic or human necessity, to the use of the fabulous to probe beyond the phenomenological, beyond appearances, beyond randomly perceived events, beyond mere history."

4. *The Fabulators* (New York, 1967), 19, 29–30.
5. Ibid., 10–11.

8

I.

FAIRY TALES,
SCRIPTURE, AND FABLE
Some Myths Revisited

Fictions are for finding things out, and they change as the
needs of sense-making change. Myths are the agents of
stability, fictions the agents of change. Myths call for
absolute, fictions for conditional assent.
— Frank Kermode, *The Sense of an Ending*

However masked it may be by symbols and images [the
fairy tale] nevertheless speaks a more direct language than
the myth or fable, for example; and children know this
instinctively, "believing" in it insofar as they find in it what
interests them most of all: an identifiable image of themselves, of their family, their parents . . . The "kingdom" of
the tale is indeed nothing else but the universe of the family, closed and clearly defined, in which the first drama of
man is played out. There is no reason to doubt that the
king of this kingdom is a husband and a father, and
nothing else . . . It may be assumed that his fabulous
wealth and power . . . are present merely to throw the
parental authority into relief; for as far as the rest is con-
cerned, it has to be admitted that we know nothing about
him. Most of the time the tale simply introduces him with
the formula "Once upon a time there was a king," then
immediately adds "who had a son . . ."
— Marthe Robert, "The Grimm Brothers"

When verbal disciplines are taught in school, two basic
modes are recognized for the appropriation and trans-
mission — simultaneously — of another's words . . . "reciting
by heart" and "retelling in one's own words." The latter

mode poses on a small scale the task implicit in all prose stylistics: retelling a text in one's own words is to a certain extent a double-voiced narration of another's words, for indeed "one's own words" must not completely dilute the quality that makes another's words unique; a retelling in one's own words should have a mixed character, able when necessary to reproduce the style and expressions of the transmitted text.
— Mikhail Bakhtin, *The Dialogic Imagination*

Fairy Tales

The mystery is within the doubleness of the heart, behind the bright façade: "The door: here they pause and catch their breath. It is heart-shaped and bloodstone-red, its burnished surface gleaming in the sunlight . . . Shining like a ruby, like hard cherry candy, and pulsing softly, radiantly. Yes, Marvelous; delicious! insuperable! but beyond: what is that sound of black rags flapping?" (*P&D*, 75). But the doubleness is within: the door that opens yields at last that ultimate mystery where we discover only ourselves.

Jack cuts down phallic stalks with an ironic sense that he has become the giant. He shamefacedly catches himself smashing the young trees, incestuously lustful for his daughter, Red Riding Hood, who is up there now taught joy by him who in "his cowardly, lonely love, [had] left out the terror" (14). His mother sits in the branches awaiting the arrival of the girl. Jack sweeps his lust under with each symbolic axe stroke ("[it] got ahold of him right now, made him grab up his axe, dig ceremonially at his crotch, and return to his labors, with a weird perverse insistence . . . But, no, it wasn't jealousy, she was his own blood, after all. And just a child" [15, 14]). But the grandmother, too, lies ruminating on lust and her jealousy of Red Riding Hood: "you warn her and it does no good I know who's got her giddy ear with his old death-cunt-and-prick songs haven't I heard them all my God . . . yes I know him well and I tell her but Granny she says Granny you don't understand the times are different . . . hah! for ain't I the old Beauty who married the Beast?" (16). Red Riding Hood comes to the cottage in midday (so often sin is performed, eyes opened under the aegis of Saint Augustine's noonday devils in these fictions), hearing the thrust of the axe strokes below, seeing all familiar, yet different:

Beyond the door? She stared at the aperture and knew: not her. No. That much was obvious, an age had passed, that much the door ajar had told her . . . the sun suddenly snapped its bonds and jerked westward, propelling her over the threshold . . . Inside, she felt the immediate oppression of the scene behind drop off her shoulders like a red cloak. All that remained of it was the sullen beat of the lumberman's axe, and she was able to still even that finally, by closing the door firmly behind her and putting the latch. (18–19)

The door closes upon the world of innocence children never really inhabit (Red Riding Hood *did* dally in the woods with the wolf), and she steps through irrevocably into that other reality that Jack had earlier tried to protect her from with his mythic fiction of innocent love. The otherness is always within us, the mirror that is every tale. Jack has become the Giant; Red Riding Hood has become her own grandmother drawn to the wolf's embrace ("she stared at the aperture and knew: not her"). All hearts are doors into the self that it may discover its own identity as the old Beauty who married the Beast. But also something beyond this role, to which we shall return.

This lamination of several familiar tales cuts through the narratives to the generational struggle that substructures all the variety of "symbols and images" individuating stories in the collection gathered by the Brüder Grimm. Externally, in Jack's aging incestuous jealousy; internally, in Red Riding Hood's detachment from that possessive desire in order to accept the reality of experience, embracing the unknown desire that is her self-discovery.

This is a reductive summary account of the opening fiction of Coover's *Pricksongs & Descants,* "The Door: A Prologue of Sorts." Prologue to the transition from innocence to experience. But also prologue to all of Coover's fiction. Jack the myth-killer has become Jack the mythologizing narrator, whose false narrative the girl leaves behind for a new reality as she steps "over the threshold." We are justified in recalling that in his "prólogo" dedicated to Cervantes later in the book, Coover told the spirit of his predecessor that "the innocence, the aura of possibility you experienced have been largely drained away, and the universe is closing in on us again. Like you, we, too, seem to be standing at the end of one age and on the threshold of another" (78), and that as fiction enters this new age it will use "familiar mythic or historical forms to combat the content of these forms and to conduct the reader . . . to the real, away from mystification to clarification, away from magic to maturity." It is a happy paradox that in *Pricksongs & Descants*, a collection of puzzling experiments in fictional narration, Coover performs just this act of conversion upon the simpler stuff of his sources. (Indeed, the collection often seems to constitute its own source study, because it is a book of fiction that is about the process of life-giving, of generation in literary as much as in psychic history.)

Let us take the revision of the fairy tale in "The Gingerbread House," a version of "Hansel and Gretel." The father is a bleaker Jack, failed in the same way, flawed in the same way, knowing in the same way. But he is a more sophisticated teller of tales, of fairy tales. His jacket is tattered, his shoes muddy, his eyes fixed: "Whether they have seen too much or too little, they betray no will to see yet more" (63). His tale-telling is a lie, a myth consciously embroidered, as Jack's was not. Jack had only given Red Riding Hood "her view of the world, in fragments of course, not really thinking it all out, she listening, he telling, and because of her gaiety and his love, his cowardly lonely love, he'd left out the terror" (14). On the other hand, the father of Hansel and Gretel (reduced by Coover to the "boy," the "girl," the "old man") "tells them a story about a good fairy who granted a poor man three wishes. The wishes, he knows, were wasted, but . . . He lengthens the tale with details about the good fairy, how sweet and kind and pretty she is, then lets the children complete the story with their own wishes, their own dreams . . . Why must the goodness of all wishes come to nothing?" (69).

But for all of the good fairy tales, the boy seems to know the dark destination of the witch's gingerbread house, toward which they are being taken; he furtively scatters an Ariadne's thread of bread crumbs. Red Riding Hood, too, when she encountered the wolf — or was it the woodsman? — in the woods "had known all along . . . Well, it would be a big production, that was already apparent. An elaborate game, embellished with masks and poetry, a marshaling of legendary doves and herbs" (18). Similarly, the girl in "Gingerbread House": "Her young gaze flicks airily from flower to flower, bird to bird, tree to tree . . . Her basket is overflowing. Does she even know the boy is dropping crumbs? or where the old man is leading them? Of course, but it's nothing! a game!" (64).

Games; with their endless possibilities for repetitions cousin-german to ritual; with their reduction of mimetic structure to the struggle among a few symbolic counters cousin-german to the familial pattern of fairy tales. But because the counters are few and repetitions of the play endless, can the players not be expected to change sides, identify their enterprise now with this counter, then with that, so that they fuse their efforts and ego now with white, now with black?

But games suggest play, and play suggests children, and children suggest innocence, and this is the set of associations in the opening paragraph of the tale:

A pine forest in the midafternoon. Two children follow an old man, dropping breadcrumbs, singing nursery tunes . . . Spots of red, violet, pale blue, gold, burnt orange. The girl carries a basket for gathering flowers. The boy is occupied with the crumbs. Their song tells of God's care for little ones. (61)

The alliterations, assonances, repetitions of phrase, staccato series such as the spots of colors seen through "filtered sunlight" carry throughout the forty-two paragraphs of the tale; the body is seen in focused and repeated parts also; eyes, hands, fingers, hearts; sunlight and darkness alternate as one passes through the woods; the gingerbread house is a cornucopia of luscious fragments: the whole is dappled beauty, almost Hopkinsesque in parts, suggestive of God's plenty for the "little ones." This surface only emphasizes, though, that the midafternoon is inexorably closing into night, and that the end of the inevitable journey is not the sweet exterior of the gingerbread house, but the door that leads within, which opened our discussion: "the door . . . It is heart-shaped and bloodstone-red . . . Shining like a ruby, like hard cherry candy, and pulsing softly, radiantly . . . but beyond: what is that sound of black rags flapping?" (75).

The sound, of course, is the witch, clutching a heart she has torn out of the breast: "She . . . lifts the heart before her eyes. The burnished heart of the dove glitters like a ruby, a polished cherry, a brilliant, heart-shaped bloodstone. It beats still. A soft radiant pulsing" (66). Formulaic repetition, then, as in the oral origins of folk tales, fairy tales, but with the difference that opposites collapse in upon one another: the symbolic dove of spiritual exhaltation and innocence (an image that plays its ambiguous role in *The Origin of the Brunists*) is identified with the door behind which lurks the witch,

13

the wolf, that "experience" which the old man already knows is inevitable, which, indeed, he embraces. At midpoint in the story we are surprised out of expected chronological context when the party seems already arrived at the house they still advance upon. The break in narrative continuity underlines, of course, the return of experience upon itself as the old man, the father, once again accepts Acrasia, Duessa, La Belle Dame sans merci, the dead temptress who lures with the symbol of life: "The witch twists and quivers, her black rags whirling, . . . From her lean bosom, she withdraws the pulsing red heart of a dove . . . Lust flattens his face and mists his old eyes, where glitter now reflections of the ruby heart. Grimacing, he plummets forward, covering the cackling witch" (68–69). To this point Coover's tale seems to accept the "content" of familiar forms, as the father joins the forces of evil, the forces of death, if reluctantly, against the children he leads to the gingerbread house. Even in embroidering his stories of the good fairy, "where," the old man poignantly wonders, "have all the good fairies gone?" (70). In the penultimate section, the old man tries one more wish, attempts to wish them back again at the beginning of the path, that they might evade the destiny closing upon them. But even should he start again, the end would be the same (the sameness realized by the narrator of "The Leper's Helix," as well as so many others in the fictions of *Pricksongs & Descants*): "But it's no use, the doves will come again, there are no reasonable wishes" (75). The good fairy is helpless to work miracles because she has herself become life petrified into the symbolic jewel that identifies dove with door: "Gossamer wings sprout from her smooth back; from her flawless chest two firm breasts with tips bright as rubies" (71).

Yet is it so simple as in fairy tales? Is the only collusion that reluctant one between father and witch? The boy, scattering the trail of crumbs which will lead them back from the game's ambiguously delightful and terrifying end goal, looks back: "The dove is a soft lustrous white, head high, breast filled . . . Only its small beak moves. Around a bread crumb . . . Doves are eating his bread crumbs. His ruse has failed" (65). In anguish, the boy falls upon the dove, the boy and girl struggle as he attempts to throttle it, and he surrounds it when the girl wrestles it free, with all the instincts of life against death. "She has thrust the dove protectively beneath her skirt, and sits, knees apart, leaning over it, weeping softly." Now the

Christian archetypes that have been hovering at the edges of the fairy tale seem about to surface as the Virgin gives life, this symbolic birth, to the Spirit. But the form here flagrantly combats its content as "the old man stoops down, lifts her bright orange apron, her skirt, her petticoats . . . The dove is nested in her small round thighs. It is dead" (67). Now all seem interchangeable with the other: The old man and the dove share betrayal of the innocents to the witch: The boy and the girl and the witch, each in his or her own way, has shared in silencing the symbolic dove. The death of innocence as the death of the spirit; this much seems clear, inenvitable: "The old man sighs and uses up a wish: he wishes his poor children well . . . but it's no use, the doves will come again, there are no reasonable wishes" (74–75).

But both of Coover's fairy tales have told us that innocence is only a myth, a lie drifted into by Jack, elaborated deliberately by the old man. Is this assumption being laid to rest both in the action and the laminated structures of these twin fictions?

As the destined trio trudge on after the discovery of the dead dove between the girl's thighs, "the body of the dove glows yet in the darkening dusk. The whiteness of the ruffled breast seems to be fighting back against the threat of night" (67–68).

In the aptly titled *Winter's Tale* Shakespeare had used the imagery shared by fairy tales and Christianity to suggest inevitably that the loss of innocence is the entrance to reality. It is, again, a play made of old tales about old tales, about generation and generations, about the symbolic entranceway from one state into the other. Speaking to his friend's wife, King Polixenes describes their childhood: "what we chang'd / Was innocence for innocence." Like "twinn'd lambs that did frisk," they would have played out life in that state but that "Temptations have since then been born to's: for / In those unfledg'd days was my wife a girl; / Your precious self had then not cross'd the eyes / Of my young playfellow" (1.2.67–79). This is not, of course, an apology, but glad acceptance of the life principle, which, "higher rear'd / With stronger blood," gives birth to the future in a play itself "so like an old tale."

The dove lives on, then, not as the white symbol of purity, but as the palpitating ruby heart of passionate life. If it eats the crumbs, it is not only because the children cannot return from the gingerbread house but also because they must not. It is, after all, the emblem of themselves, of their discovery of each other and that merging into the otherness archetypically expressed in the sweet terrors of sex. Exaggerating, embellishing the buried images of the Brüder Grimm, Coover plays preposterously with that incestuous love game that began with our first innocent parents (Eve was, after all, flesh of Adam's bone):

The boy climbs up on the chocolate roof to break off a peppermint-stick chimney, comes sliding down . . . The girl, reaching out to catch him in his fall, slips on a sugarplum and tumbles gaily into a sticky rock garden of candied chestnuts. Laughing gaily, they lick each other clean. And how grand is the red-and-white striped chimney the boy holds up for her; how bright! how sweet! But the door: . . . Oh, what a thing is that door! Shining like a ruby, like hard cherry candy, and pulsing softly, radiantly! (75)

Beyond, of course, behind the door is the "sound of black rags flapping." But it is only the old Beauty who married the Beast, the terror of experience. After all, the good fairy offers only dead magic, her wings and ruby-tipped breasts tinsel left over from the symbolic green room of Coover's sources. The witch holds the palpitating heart of passion, which lures across the threshold into maturity.

Walt Disney first debased the fairy tale into cartoon, caricature, with his treatment of Snow White; later he would make a similar vandal's raid upon Pinocchio (this latter an incursion that Coover will repulse in *The Public Burning*). Disney's theft was so unpleasant that it became an obscene symbol for years, available as a Hollywood memorabilium for thousands of tourists who took home the popular poster of the dwarves' gangbang. Coover's treatment in "The Dead Queen" incorporates the poster's action and implications into what is one of his clearest early distinctions between popular literature and its incorporation into a *dialogic* structure (we shall come to terms with this term later).

Coover's narrator is the Prince who weds Snow White.[1] The narrative is easy, unconfused. It begins with the burial of the Queen in the mountain cave, where the dwarves have worked their vein of gold. The Prince wonders at this ritualistic anachronism: "Why are we burying her in the mountain? We no longer believe in underworlds nor place hope in moldering kings, still we stuff them back into the earth's navel, as though anticipating some future interest"

1. *Quarterly Review of Literature* 18, no. 3-4 (1973): 304-13.

(308). So much, apparently, for continuities, miracles, regeneration. But the Prince's puzzlement is the insistent factor: philosophic, hapless Hamlet caught in a farce peopled by archetypes, dwarves, and doubts, he watches the gnomes tumble down the mountain. The narrative cuts back to his own experience of his wedding banquet on the previous night. Everyone drank, the Queen performed her death dance in the red-hot iron shoes, he observed Snow White's inability to discern the horror, he bedded her in a turmoil of obscene competition with the dwarves, who undermined all romance with their lubricious acrobatics as they took Snow White in every position for the thousandth time, and he awoke from his nightmare, in ultimate sexual triumph over these satyrs but "spent, to find no blood on the nuptial linens" (309). This flashback in the midsection of the story reflects old traditional dramatic incongruities, which themselves reflected the merger of realism, romance, and folk legend. Here, as in the *commedia dell'arte scenarii* of the Renaissance, the young lovers, beautifully costumed and dictioned *inamorati*, play out their love idyll against a backdrop of obscene interruption from Harlequin, Pantalone, the spirits of lust and disorder from the city of society on one hand (fathers, dukes, and kings) and the underworld of demons on the other. But the grotesque comedy of the wedding night gives way again to the primal scene of the mountain burial, and to the Prince's reflections upon the nature of the drama in which he is a character. He believes the Queen has orchestrated the entire movement, from the moment she faced the mirror and sent Snow White to her doom with the hunter ("or perhaps there had been no Hunter at all, perhaps it had been that master of disguises, the old Queen herself" [309]): "We've all been reduced to jesters, fools; tragedy she reserved for herself alone . . . poisoned us all with pattern" (306). And that venom has resulted in reducing even this Prince, so intent upon "finding things out," to a member of a troupe of mythic comedians, unwilling agents of stability: "the old Queen — what she had lusted for was a part in the story, immortality, her place in guarded time . . . Even our names were lost, she'd transformed us into colors, simple proclivities, our faces were forever fixed and they weren't even our own" (305).

Yet, once thinking upon pattern, one comes to that impasse of myth which leads simultaneously to doubt and belief. "This seemed true, but so profoundly true, it seemed false" (306). This is the inscrutability of all myths, all absolutes: "A pity the old Queen had arrived so late, died so soon, missed our dedicated fulfillment of her comic design — or perhaps this, too, was part of her tragedy, the final touch to a life shaped by denial" (306–7). So much for doubt, for the Prince of indecision.

But "The Dead Queen" is a fiction, in both Coover's and Frank Kermode's vocabularies, although its source and its narrator are mythic, with all of the assent to magic absolutes implicit in that category. As he watches the glass box, once the enchanted Snow White's prison, now the Queen's coffin, the Prince reflects upon the terribly permanent innocence of feeling which Snow White has revealed, her inability to go beyond the door ("No, I thought, she's suffered no losses, in fact that's just the trouble, that hymen can never be broken, not even by me, not in a thousand nights, this is her gift and essence, and because of it she can see neither before nor aft, doesn't even know there is a mirror on the wall" [305]). But turning from Snow White's frigid innocence, the Prince, immature Platonist, fantasizes another absolute, imagines that magic exists behind that door that leads to maturity.

I gazed at her in her glass coffin . . . I was beginning to appreciate her subtlety, and so assumed that this, too, had been part of her artifice, a lingering hope for her own liberation, she'd used the mirror as a door, tried to . . . Of course, there were difficulties in such a perfect view of things, she was dead, for example, but one revelation was leading to another, and it came to me suddenly that maybe the old Queen had loved me, had died for *me*! I, too, was prone to linger at still pools, listen to the flattery of soothsayers, organize my life and others' by threes and sevens. (312)

It is a mad, narcissistic rationality innate in one born into the patterns of myth which will flourish unexpectedly in the coincidences encountered by Richard Nixon as he puzzles the meaning of his destiny as it crosses that of Ethel Rosenberg in *The Public Burning*. In "The Dead Queen" it draws the Prince into the dissolution of his own dreams as he kisses the Queen's corpse hoping to resurrect her. "She stank and her blue mouth was rubbery and cold as a dead squid. I'd been wrong about her, wrong about everything." The king turns away in disgust, Snow White faints, the Prince perseveres, kissing the corpse again, tumbling it from its magic glass coffin, then, still absolute for the magic within pattern, "Maybe a third time," he cries, but "Guards restrained me." The father-King turns away. The dwarves are up to their usual lively obscenities, "reviving Snow White by fanning her skirts." The corpse is summarily stuffed back in the box and buried. Myth and magic are gone, with all the lure of absolutes by which fairy tales such as "Snow White" "transform us into colors" and so join with those ubiquitous Platonic myths that reduce us to "simple proclivities." The Beautiful is the Good is the True. Having played out his role, like Adam and Eve, the Prince turns his back upon lost innocence to enter the world; finding things out, he has crossed the line from myth into fiction, accepting the change implicit in that choice: "I turned and walked down the mountain. Thinking: if this is the price of beauty, it's too high. I was glad she was dead" (313).

Coover in these stories accepts and preserves the integrity of the narrative history presented him in his folk sources. The significant difference is in the place of the narrator. "Red Riding Hood," "Hansel and Gretel," "Snow White" — children's tales (one could fairly interpolate here, "all myths") are told from the voice of authority: "Once upon a time *there was.*" But only the narrator knew that time, and it is the child's absolute abdication to that absolute authority that remakes the merely typical, recurrent pattern of experience into an article of faith, the typical become archetypical, the patterned become magic, mythic. Coover reworks these narratives from within, the narrative voice always emergent from the participants themselves as they work through their own limited destinies within the larger patterns to a perception that the pattern itself is limited, dubious, its meaning indiscernible. And with this discovery, character and reader are thrown back upon the resources of individual action.

Scriptures

The "kingdom" of the tale is indeed nothing else but the universe of the family, closed and clearly defined, in which the first drama of man is played out. There is no reason to doubt that the king of this kingdom is a husband and a father, and nothing else.

— Marthe Robert, "The Grimm Brothers"

But as the days of Noah were, so shall also the coming of
the Son of man be. For as in the days that were before the
flood they were eating and drinking, marrying and giving
in marriage, until the day that Noah entered into the ark,
and knew not until the flood came and took them all
away; so shall also the coming of the Son of man be.
— Matt. 24:37-39

Robert's observation of the radically familial structure of fairy
tales, so useful a cue in watching Coover reshape materials from that
source, can direct us to the heart of another vein of myth which
threads through the shorter fictions into Coover's first novel, *The
Origin of the Brunists*. For the structural images upon which Christianity is built are no less firmly rooted in the formulae of the family.
There is the Father, the Son, the Mother. In his treatment of fairy
tales, Coover found it necessary to reconstruct the patterns of generational relationship so that the children shared or even precipitated a
collusion by which they accepted experience as a species of self-meta-
morphosis into the roles of their elders. In Christian myth there is no
such necessity. The transcendent taxonomy that gives the myth its
absolute authority has already made the Son only an aspect of the
Father, regenerated and regenerative in the social world as a Spirit
both generations share. But as the Father's divine incarnation, the
Son himself becomes the authority figure, the husband who is therefore implicit and potential father: "the head of every man is Christ;
and the head of the woman is the man; and the head of Christ is
God" (1 Cor. 11:3). The Mother is, by miracle rather than maturity,
also the Virgin; and by spiritual marriage of ourselves to Christ, the
body to the head of the Church, we all become brethren under God,
admonished to add "to brotherly kindness, charity" (2 Pet. 1:7).

But, again, Coover reexamines the taxonomy by removing the
voice of authority from the narratives it offers him. His scriptural fictions recount the familiar phenomena of transcendent miracles from
the puzzled perspective of the human participants who, not en-
cumbered by the entire arc of Christian pattern, are unable or not apt
to infer good news from the dread and irony of their own experience.
These are historical beings caught up in the crotch of a nasty stick
that only distanced chroniclers could possibly discern as a divining

rod for the sources of glory which, we are told, in human relations translate into "brotherly kindness, charity."

"The Brother" is spoken by a narrator whose origins appear anything but scriptural. He speaks a pages-long account of surprise in what at first must seem pseudo-southern Americanese, Snopsean discourse in dialect and, one might guess from the opening, also in plot:

Right there right there in the middle of the damn field he says he wants to put that thing together him and his buggy ideas and so me I says "how the hell you going to get it down to the water?" but he just focuses me out sweepin the blue his eyes rollin like they do when he gets het on some new lunatic notion and he says not to worry none about that just would I help him for God's sake. (*P&D*, 92)

The narrative continues less than develops, recounted in the twang of the frontier no less obviously than within the exasperated confines of familial obligation. The project is a boat constructed in a landlocked countryside, "and it ain't no goddamn fishin boat he wants to put up neither in fact it's the biggest damn thing I ever heard of." The narrator's wife is pregnant; his work in helping his brother and nephews build the incredible ark is forcing more and more farming effort upon the wife, who "can't see why you always have to be babying that old fool," but "packs me some sandwiches just the same and some sandwiches for my brother" in a sort of sisterly "kindness, charity." This brother is a species of natural, ambiguously impervious to the plight of the narrator and of his wife: Reminded of the sacrifices he is demanding,

he just sighs long and says "no it just don't matter" and he sits him down on a rock kinda tired and stares off and looks like he might even for God's sake cry and so I go back to bringin wood up to him and he's already started on the keel and frame God knows how *he* ever found out to build a damn boat . . . Lord he was twenty when I was born and the first thing I remember was havin to lead him around so he didn't get kicked by a damn mule. (93)

The ark finished, the rains begin. The narrator and his wife share a happy romantic idyll as (admiring the crib the father-to-be has carved from wood left over from the ark) they toast the crops that the rain will release, along with the baby now felt imminent in her womb, and they joke about the brother's folly. As the rains continue, fright sets in. The wife objects out of pride, but the narrator insists upon seeking refuge in the enormous boat.

> And the LORD said, I will destroy man whom I have created from the face of the earth . . . for it repenteth me that I have made them. But Noah found grace in the eyes of the LORD . . .
> Noah was a just man and perfect.
> — Gen. 6.7–9

The tears the narrator sensed in his brother's mood may have been a reaction to the desperate task of turning his back upon mankind, which was Noah's burden from the Lord; or, they may have been the feeling projection of a charitable brother. In any case, when the narrator stands in the whipping rains to ask asylum on the ark, the brother turns away:

Still he don't say a damn word he just raises his hand in that same sillyass way and I holler "hey you stupid sonuvabitch I'm soaking wet goddamn it and my house is fulla water and my wife she's about to have a kid and she's apt to get sick all wet and cold to the bone and I'm askin' you —" and right then right while I'm still talking he turns around and he goes back in the boat and I can't hardly believe it me his brother but he don't come back out.

Is the myth of "brotherly kindness, charity," then, a mere myth in another sense? There is no answer in Coover's rebuilding of the ark, only the ambivalent inferences of a man trapped between absolute mysteries and human miseries.

> I can't see my brother's boat no more gone just water how _how_ did he know? that bastard and yet I gotta hand it to him it's not hard to see who's crazy around here I can't see my house no more I just left my wife inside where I found her I couldn't hardly stand to look at her the way she was.
> — P&D, 98

The ambivalence persists in Coover's other revisions of scriptural myths, but the balance of credibility shifts further away from the transcendent perspective of the source toward the human vantage point from which the participants must attempt to understand

events. The most effective of these is "J's Marriage," a first version of
the Immaculate Conception, a Christian mystery to which Coover
will return in the play "A Theological Position."[2]

"J" is much older than the virgin he pursues with "adoration." He is
experienced, a would-be cynic contemplating the "ultimate misery of
any existence, the inevitable disintegration of love" (112). But for all
of this he courts the virgin ardently. The ardor reveals within her a
radical terror of sex:

a fear which no doubt cowered beneath the surface all the time, but which
had always been placated by the suspicion that J himself was really nothing
more physically substantial than his words, words which at times pierced the
heart, true, kindled the blood, powerful words, even at times painful; but
their power and their pain did not, *could* not pin one helplessly to the earth,
could not bring actual blood. (112–13)

But their power is sufficient to bring her to marriage, and J is con-
vinced that he can patiently, gradually overcome her. The word and
the world, as always, badly married. Their wedding night was a time
of poignant beauty, understanding exchanged through hours of fully
clothed embraces until in the dawn J watched her fall asleep as he
kneaded her temples. "J wept again to realize the meaning and the
importance of her sleep." It is a poignant phrase, a rich and ambiguous fulcrum upon which the history of the marriage turns. Time
brings advances and retreats, and a joy for J which transcends, in
part perhaps emanates from, his frustration. Then that night arrives
toward which J's patient will has been bent from the beginning: he
enters the bedroom to find his wife standing in the stunning beauty
of her nakedness for the first time. Overwhelmed, he embraces,
caresses her, but, at the penultimate moment of anticipation, "I am
expecting a baby, she said." Stunned anew, nonetheless J listens as

she explained to him simply that her pregnancy was an act of God, and he
had to admit against all mandates of his reason that it must be so, but he
couldn't imagine whatever had brought a God to do such a useless and, well,
yes, in a way, vulgar thing . . . it was simply unimaginable to him that any
God would so involve himself in the tedious personal affairs of this or any
other human animal, so inutterably unimportant were they to each other.
(117)

2. "The Reunion" (*Iowa Review* 1, no. 4 [Fall 1970]: 64–67) is something of a
halfway house toward these later fictions. It recounts Jesus' postresurrection return
to the disciples and its gruesome aftermath.

When the wife gives birth, J has a mystic moment in which finally he sees the meaning of existence; a moment "which he later renounced, needless to say, later understood in the light of his overwrought and tortured emotions." From that moment the arc of the marriage descends rapidly; J loses all interest in, all contact with, the wife ("in later years J found himself incapable even of describing her to himself or any other person"); the boy and J share a "complete indifference" to each other. "Just as well; J grew to prefer not being bothered to any other form of existence." With this stage, one realizes that J shares with his withdrawn God difference and detachment from his creatures.

As J ages, only one event pierces this indifference: the recollection that may, indeed, have been only a dream, that one night after the child's birth, after bathing the breasts of his nursing wife, he had penetrated her in sleep. Only that punctuates a growing senility until the moment of his death, when he collapses into a glass of red wine, with a last memory that gives resonance to her fear of the physical, "actual blood," to a ludicrous semisuggestion of the Eucharist that is the blood of the divine child, a being otherwise so nearly excluded from the story. The father dying awash with the symbolic blood of the mythic child: We have come full circle back to Coover's familial fairy tales by way of the central mystery of the Christian myth. As we were earlier reminded in that other context: "the 'kingdom' of the tale is indeed nothing else but the universe of the family . . . There is no reason to doubt that the king of this kingdom is a husband and a father, and nothing else."

But which father? The Christian myth had robbed Joseph of his paternity; in concluding "J's Marriage," Coover demystifies the miracle as J (is Jehovah, after all, only Joseph?) recaptures, harmonizes that long-lost fatherhood. Dying, he reinterprets "the meaning and the importance of her sleep" in the dawn long ago:

He had a rather uncharacteristic thought about the time she, the wife, fell asleep, or apparently so, that morning following the wedding night; he laughed (that high-pitched rattle of old men), startling the person who had been listening, and died as described above. (119)

Later Coover dramatized the triangulation inherent in the immaculate conception in the play "A Theological Position." A priest, acting as theologian for The Church, has come to a peasant couple.

The inscrutably smiling woman, the husband reports, has conceived without penetration. In the event, the husband subverts the mythic conception as J had done in the earlier story. The priest's theology makes it imperative that the woman be penetrated in order that neither reason nor mythology be outraged. The man induces the priest to mount her; he succeeds only by the proxy stimulation of sensual polysyllabic words — to discover that she is no virgin. The denouement again depends upon the powerlessness of language once it has been diverted into the closed channels of myth. Much in the play is awkward, as is the titular pun, reflecting the woman's final sacrifice to the empty rhythms of the Eucharist as she lies spread upon a pseudo-altar.[3] But if words have a radical relationship to both sexuality and impotence in their power for the characters caught up in Coover's scriptural fictions, for J's wife no less than for the priest of "A Theological Position," it is their confluence into primal archetypes which the latter articulates. As the priest begins to mount the woman, he realizes "that this has all happened before, in a way, . . . I've imagined, . . . I've often had dreams . . ." "Fantasies," the husband explains, and the priest Christianizes the observation: "Or aspirations. Mythogenetic visions . . . It's a way . . . of apprehending the transcendental." Well, maybe. But before he was bewitched by the woman's flesh, the priest had known that not only this latest version, but all miracles of immaculate conception are "wishful fantasies of the peasant imagination . . . you people simply lack the historical knowledge to put such things as giants and fairies in perspective."

This little play, then, is a fabliau about the family which brings us again to "The Door."[4]

Fable

The priest listens to words, idler as authoritative audience. As critic, commentator. He and Jack, and the father of Hansel and Gretel, find themselves trapped in the generic structure of myth as revealed

3. One hears the echo of Leo Taxil's antimythic joke about Joseph's query to Mary concerning her pregnancy, as reported in Joyce's *Ulysses*: "Que [sic] vous a mis dans cette fichue position?" Her response might alert us to the ambiguous dove that plays so large a role in "The Gingerbread House" and *The Origin of the Brunists*: "C'est le pigeon, Joseph."

4. The tradition goes back to the medieval fabliau "Du chevalier qui fist les cons

through a form of tale which crossed over into the bestiality of the "fable": a form escaped only by the female figures, "beauty" always escaping the moral by embracing the beast.

The author bids a respectful adieu to old Cervantes in the "prólogo" and finds himself Cervantes. The girl walks through the door more sagacious than her jealous begetter. The old woman joins Jack in thinking that the girl must learn what she already knows. The universal syntax of the tale structure has taught her the role she plays in this incestuous family circle of beauties and beasts: She knows her own myth. She has been behind the door before, in that sense. But now she has arrived before it as merely her self, a girl whose palpable being demystifies all roles. This is a doubleness that will be expanded in the orgiastic ritual concluding *The Universal Baseball Association, Inc.* But like the sacrificial Damon of that novel, Red Riding Hood accepts the reality of both role and self. She will become her own grandmother, Beauty sacrificed in the Beast's bed, become focus of that delusion (or disillusionment) whence myths seem to step into another dimension to acquire and pass on a pattern of meaning. Yet she is, like Damon, a player, a passenger across the threshold of sensuality into that existential life, which is the only thing she wants from all these imposed patterns. The grandmother's "wisdom," Jack's terror, the exegetical words the priest has learned finally will descend upon her like the weight of the red cloak. But for now it has dropped off her shoulders. As the young ballplayer/victim of J. Henry Waugh's mythic imagination will say: "'It's not a trial . . . It's not even a lesson. It's just what it is.' Damon holds the baseball up between them. It is hard and white and alive in the sun."

> "The Rosenbergs have been. . . . Talking and, acting like characters out of Aesop's Fables or something." "Knowing that Aesop was around to write it down."
> — *PB*, 409

The young can feel their separate beings in this high noon sun, the warmth of it an echo of the blood firing the feeling, inducing them to make that Faustian pact with the future wherein they become mere

---

parle": see R. H. Bloch, "The Fabliaux, Fetishism, and Freud's Jewish Jokes," *Representations* 4 (1983): 14–15.

myth, role, avatar for the next generation of springtime's players. The pact is made with all the knowledge that myth has forgotten: that the blood and the sun are warm and more real than words. But "deep in the gloom of the forest, the old lion lies dying in his cave" (1). At the end there are two kinds of death; the first is that of the pact, the acceptance of the inevitable mythic role. But at the end there is also the existential self who has felt the sun and knows that mythic kingdoms are shit: "His ancient hide drapes the royal bones like a worn blanket, rheum clots his warm nose, his eyes are dimmed with cataracts. Yet, even in such decline, the familiar hungers stir in him still" (1).

In "Aesop's Forest" an older Coover imagines the end even of the myth of literary transcendency, the moment when the power of persuasion, like all those others both more and less personal, dies ("the familiar hunger stirs in him still, . . . his appetite for power outlasting his power to move, his need for raw flesh" [1]). "The Door" opened upon feeling, upon role, upon their impossible inseparability, incompatibility. Myth and Being; Beauty and the Beast. And to that Coover returns, in the grotesque guise of the writer as lion, fox, and sacrificial victim.

Coover's choice of vehicle for the writer's dilemma of self-immolation could not be bettered. Let us contrast Aesop with Cervantes, who created in Quijote the creator of a fiction that moved from those mythic types he had been reading into an existential world of belated knight-errantry which never existed, and yet was more real than its sources had ever been. Quijote created a real world in which others could participate in preference to the modern social strictures that at first designated him mad. His compatriots, Sancho Panza, the scholar, the priest, begged him not to die because that madness of the word-inspired Don had turned Rozinante into their Pegasus — he was, like his sources, a mythologist, but he was living this lie as an author, insinuating it into the lives of all the others he met as the initial absurdities gave way to the universal theater of part two.

Behind this, Cervantes is enigmatic. We do not know if he knew in the beginning, guessed, that what seemed another Renaissance satire of generic form (*las historias*) would become a new gradually realized genre, in whatever terms these questions might have been available to him. But in any event Cervantes' situation in relation to his work was traumatically divorced from that of Aesop. Cervantes was the writer in the sense of one who commanded a world.

But Aesop is a creature of writing, his writing, the avatar of the need for myth. The fable involving beasts (not all of his do, nor do Coover's) precedes the collection under Aesop's name.[5] It has analogues everywhere, but it only becomes a genre in the Greek age of self-consciousness, and genres need authority, an author, an Aesop. We hear varying rumors of him as slave, as king's emissary, as Thersitean satirist, as mythic gobbo from Herodotus, Heraclides, Plutarch, Aristophanes. He may have existed or may have been a name created by a genre, a need to give a forest of strange beasts and their stories an author. Should there be no author, the stories would recede into the inexplicable distance without mythic structure, without beginning, an unthinkable preface to fables whose applicability was without end. And the structure, of course, was again familial, but this time in that way that animal masking permits: the family as treachery. The lion and the fox were the symbiotic symbols of power for a deposed Machiavelli, and he borrowed them from that recurrent pair of pretenders in Aesop's collection of fables. Coover sees that they could be combined to define and destroy the author's mythic role as "creator." Quijote, displaced image of the word-crazed writer as mad god (J. Henry Waugh with his league records is not an isolated phenomenon), demystifies his world through death. Once the creative act has been elected, an inner world projected into others' space, there is no other way to end it. It is as preposterous to try to rewind the skein of imagined worlds as to renounce any other act of birth. Filicide is a form of suicide. So it may well have been in most literal form in the case of Aesop. We have only the evidence of an early Aristophanic scholiast and of Plutarch that Aesop was killed by the Delphians for sacrilege (or satire — the case is indeterminate in the accounts[6]) by being hurled from the sacred rock Hyampus, reciting the apologue to the fable of "The Tortoise and the Eagle" at his death; that is, the moral for one who would fly into competition with the gods. But the fable itself may have been the source of the story of Aesop's death, otherwise not mentioned: The tortoise begged

5. The literature is enormous and repetitive. I employ the text and introduction to Emile Chambry's edition: *Ésope, Fables* (Paris, 1927).
6. Chambry, xi–xiv.

the eagle to teach him flight; the eagle remonstrated, then, succumbing to the tortoise's insistence, carried him aloft and dropped him. The writer's death recorded through a myth of his own invention: So it may have been historically, and so Coover seizes upon this inevitable paradox in "Aesop's Forest," interweaving the death of Aesop with the death of the tortoise. That is the way fable becomes myth. But the fabulist hunchback (that, too, perhaps a late myth adapted from the fable of Zeus's judgment that the ingrate tortoise must carry his home upon his back) and the falling tortoise are interwoven by Coover into the last fable that Aesop never wrote: that of the Liebestod of fox and lion, Aesop and the forest of his creation.

In Coover's fable about Aesop's fables, the lion is dying, not feigning. But he is also reconsidering his relationship to the kingdom he has made the forest imagine — the kingdom and himself as king, as source, as truth; the fox as inevitable ally, alter ego, antagonist: the fox chosen because no one would trust him among the lion's would-be heirs: "A sigh rips through him like the windy echo of some half-remembered rage: his hatred of duplicity . . . he was once the source of all their truths, now, crippled, sinking into dry rot, reduced to begging from a thieving liar, he still is: it is truth itself that is changing. Yes, yes, he thinks, we take *everything* with us when we go" (2).

This the old beauty, then, who, for all his self-justifications, loves the foxy beast. But what has his life been, what has the fox's life been but "juicy morals for the hunchback's fables"? (2). Crippled, creator of surly order, king dying down into the role of clown, he knows he is Aesop's creation. But also his double, as both prepare for death. Maybe the lion says it, maybe the fabulist, maybe Coover, but "death is everywhere in Aesop's dark forest" (3), as it was in the woods of Hansel and Gretel's desire. The speaker has compressed all the fables into raw terms that laminate Aesop's varied morals into a single pattern for which they were never intended ("Eagles and vixens devour each other's young, newborn apes are murdered by their mothers, hens by serpents they themselves have hatched"; "Even lions" [3]).

But there is the fox and the fabulist, voyeurs and participants in this naïve king's dream. How did the lion come by his crippled age, but as avatar of the crippled Aesop? How did Aesop come by his mastery, but as avatar of the lion, king of the beasts? And how did they survive but by the lie:

With the fox things are not always what they seem, . . . The fabler watches the watchers watch . . . In him something more fundamental is dying with the dying lion, . . . even the strongest become the playthings of cowards: this is the message . . . in the fox's grinning jaws. And it enrages him. Not the message, but the grin. It is his the fabler's, own. (5)

As the story is retold, the lion is dying in his den while the fox watches. Of course, it is Aesop who watches the watcher, watches his bifurcation of self as writer (lie and truth, fox and lion, in uneasy alliance at the mouth of the cave). But Aesop knows only enough to not know his creation's insight into himself, into origins. He is the peeping tom of his own forest: "Two eyes in particular absorb his gaze: the dark squinty lopsided orbs of the little brown humpback, come to hurl himself like a clown into the final horror — for isn't it the cripple who always wants to lead off the dance?" (5). The myth begins, as always, in the half-man, "the grotesque grotesqued" (5). But neither fabulist nor his beasts are capable of the lie, even about the lying essence of the fox. It is a little history of this permanent aspect of metaphor: the story Coover tells of how Aesop, the lion, and the fox all die together. They are, after all, of the same birth: "we take *everything* with us when we go." The lion knew that, knew that the forest was rife with death at his dying. This is the truth that the lion knows and that Aesop, come to join his creature, only half-intuits, because "in him, something more fundamental is dying with the dying lion, and just when he needs it most . . . this is what he fears to lose, even as he's losing it — his ruthless solitude" (4). Aesop is dying, too, in another way: The Delphians are seeking him as a sacrilegious criminal; the lion's cave, his own literary forest, will be his last hiding place before they cast him off the cliff. In both he is not alone, lion and fabulist have created a mythic kingdom that must come to an end, cripples who made myths of glory read in the sorry hieroglyphs of the real world: "Much of this the fabler reads in all the shit he squats and tumbles in: the hard nuggets of avidity and pride, puddled funk, noisome pretense, the frantic scatter of droppings unloosed on the run in uncertainty and confusion — the eloquent text of the forest floor" (7). But to *read* this text, to seize its meaning, that is the unlikely act of creation. Aesop remembers a costly joke he made about why "we so often turned around to examine our own turds," and becomes serious about this metaphoric act of marriage between the mere life and meaning, mortal and myth: "The real reason we look back of course is to gaze for a moment in awe and wonder at what we've made — it's the closest we ever come to being at one with the gods" (7) — or, he might have added, with the beasts.

But then there is the tortoise, falling through space as Aesop watches the lion and fox, the earthbound thing orgulous of flight into the heavens — the author/god as suicidal fool flapping his little feet as wings carrying him, like the others, to death on the forest floor, thinking about the end of aspiration, of the lie and the loneliness as he hurtles into self-knowledge: "Why has that goddamn eagle left him up here — flap! flap! flap! — *all alone?*" (13). It will soon be Aesop's fate; they find him in the temple "as though he'd come here to our city *seeking* to die" (18); they drag him to the cliff of retribution. The tortoise falls, Aesop is cornered, the fox lies and laughs at the lion. Tempting the stag a second time into the lion's cave, the fox steals the heart that the lion coveted, and taunts the dying king about the realities between bites: "'You can stop looking, he didn't have one,' he'd told the motheaten old geezer, with his mouth full, 'anybody who'd come twice into a lion's den . . . has to be ninety percent asshole, and that's what you just ate'" (6). The fox as liar has gotten to the heart of the matter, cynical mythologist, hunter of the simple-minded lion or stag, purveyor of fables that lie like truth. Beneath contempt, but beyond disillusion, the fox is so knowing that the lion can trust him because no one can ally himself to such powers of unfettered insight. The lion trusts this fox, then, with a last secret, which is the way to kill the lion quickly when the time comes ("We're going to let you play the hero" [16], the lion says, but one wonders who else may be encompassed by this royal we; has he too been reading the fabulist's forest floor?). The tortoise falls, philosophizing on theories of flight; the fox eats, watches, sneers; Aesop nears the cliff edge; the lion staggers to the cave mouth as the forest comes alive with blood lust: "Death is everywhere in Aesop's dark forest." The tortoise hurtles by the half-blind king, "something whistles past his ear and explodes — SPLAT! — beside him, startling him just enough to tip him over" (20). So much for the philosopher of high flight. But the lion rights himself, forges into the last battle against, with, his creatures, or Aesop's — who can tell with these liars who keep inventing one another ("there are no limits any longer," it is rumored throughout the forest, "that's the message of the old king's desperate condition, this point-headed freak's [Aesop] intrusion here" [8]); "the

fox lies stretched out across the cave mouth, as though to define certain boundaries, or invent them" (9); but the lesser beasts are right,
the invention has failed, and the lion reminds the fabulist in their last
interview that "turtles want to fly, too . . ." but Aesop grasps at a
last mythic straw, which the lion breaks: "'Impossible,' (Aesop
asserts) 'There's a barrier . . . ' At least there *was* . . . Has it
somehow been breached?" And the lion answers from his creator's
own repertoire of fallacious wisdom: "'If there's a moral to be had,
fabler, it can be done'" (11).

The lion goes forth to meet "all the fabled terrors and appetites of
the mortal condition, drawn together here now for one last de-
mented frolic. The forest is literally atwinkle with that madness that
attends despair" (5). The lion moves toward his threshold as Red
Riding Hood had done, and the beasts leap upon him through the
broken barrier of myth — but like the girl's transition into youth, the
lion's transition into death is an existential glory. Tusks sink into
him, bees buzz in his ear, he is being eviscerated, "his last delicious
moment on earth, and it's the most fun he's had since he sneezed a
cat" (21). Well tutored, the fox comes at this moment; the lion
remonstrates that it is too early to finish him, the fox giggles and
bites his jugular as the lion slashes him from heart to groin, and they
die, "their organs mingling like scrambled morals" (22).

And the Delphians have Aesop on the cliff. Fabulist still, "he
cocked his head impudently to one side. 'Let me tell you a story,' he
said. Ye gods, the little freak was incorrigible" (19). Aesop's first tale
to his pursuers is one Coover has carefully saved from his retellings
of the Aesopean canon, a story of the Delphians' asinine behavior.
But the last is a tale of incest, of a father who fucked his daughter. He
flaps his stunted arms in imitation of the turtle and leaps with a laugh
as the lion and fox embrace in death. As the lion remembers the
mythologist wilfully, wistfully, who has been as much his creature as
creator, born as they were of one imaginative act of bad faith. Incestuous father and child, leaving the philosophic turtle to die tangled in
his sytematic art of reasoning. But lion and fabulist must make one
with the fox, that liar who always knew the limits of story, of its
origins in the forest where Jack strikes down the young trees, Red
Riding Hood pursues the wolf — and ideals remain mingled with
blood and the organs of begetting and dying: "It's all shit anyway,"
the lion seems to hear the fox "grunt as his spine snaps — one final

treachery! He feels as though he's falling, and he only wishes, hanging on as the light dies and the earth spins, that his friend the fabler were here to whisper in his ear, the one without the bees in it, one last word, not so much of wisdom, as of communion . . . as the forest extinguishes itself around him" (22).[7]

"The Door" led Coover through two decades to "Aesop's Forest." The two woods, antipastoral along with others his creatures inhabited, drew into their problematic treatment of myth those other scriptural landscapes, drew all mythologizing into question, as would Coover's treatment of games, of politics. Or did they? Could Red Riding Hood or the new Aesop's lion have life without the liar, the grotesque voyeur who seems to the forest made only of eyes and words? It may all be shit anyway, but the world's soul is made of its body's augurers.

The precursor of grotesque Aesop lies twenty or more years before in Coover's fictive career, another satyr on a not-quite-deserted island, the "caretaker's son" of "The Magic Poker," which initiates the storytelling, demystifying stories of *Pricksongs & Descants* after "The Door" has opened upon the experience of re-creating the self as role and disinvolving the self from that role. All pastoral had done it; "Morris in Chains" did homage to the satyr/scribbler as escapee from society into genre. But he was too involved to long escape; not so the caretaker's son, his hairy tuft of imagination left over from a genre abandoned and rediscovered, a beast recognizing the value of fabling:

I wander the island, inventing it. I make a sun for it, and trees . . . I deposit shadows and dampness . . . and scatter ruins . . . All gutted and window-busted and autographed and shat upon. I impose a hot midday silence, . . . But anything can happen. (20)

The stuff of art has always been fetid, carnage and shit. This is what the lion knows. But the humpback fabulist (was that not always the image of fertility?) and caretaker left over after the deflowering of the forest, the hero in the ruins, knows better, knows it is better to fly upside down than to roar the mere sense of self. As Aesop said, looking back at the shit we write is as close as we come to the gods. This is why flight and falling are the same. Something like this is

---

7. Coover deliberately ignores the resurrection myths that became attached to Aesop (ibid., xvii–xviii).

Coover's aesthetic, into which, as we shall see, American mythology, personified as Richard Nixon, sticks its foot.

This reminder brings us to the crossroads I mentioned in the introduction to these meditations and readings, readings of a novelist and meditations upon the form itself. We must discern the interrelationships and the differences, the barriers between fiction and metafiction, between pornography (or ritual) and romance.

Clearly, in the tales and fables I have selected to represent Coover's practice of the forms of shorter fiction, our attention has been upon the act of writing. And the writer has been center stage through much of the discourse — Cervantes is placed at the literal center of *Pricksongs & Descants* in Coover's dialogue with their shared problems, the problematic by which myth gets remade into fiction. The lion is the hero, or antihero, but Aesop is the protagonist of "Aesop's Forest." But all writing is not about writing. Or, rather, if it is, much of the best has learned the pact of Red Riding Hood and the lion: The novel must be news as well as expected form, conformation. One has one life to live in fiction as in fact; fiction transcends pattern because of its integrity, even as it can be flattened into roles, repetitions. But these repetitions are the guarantors of recognition, the indispensable challenge to individual accomplishment, that beyond which one must imagine. And nowhere are they more restrictive than in those two superficially disjunctive worlds, that of pornography and that of games. The formulae for each is numerical, the combinations quickly exhausted. Coover has always been fascinated by the absurd conjunction: in *The Origin of the Brunists*, a numerologist's mad orgy, the moment of destiny strikes while a young couple couple in a car outside a basketball court. Lucky Pierre has tried every sexual position to become, at last, voyeur of his filmed self in endless repetition. Gloomy Gus learns sex as he learns football, by the numbers. As Hettie says while fucking Henry, "Oh, that's a game, Henry! *That's* really a *great* old *game!*"

In this light, let us watch the novel become a story of play transcending game, of fiction escaping the fabulist. But in *The Universal Baseball Association, Inc., J. Henry Waugh, Prop.*, if the text is about writing, about games, numbers, genres, it is also about how (Aesop) one writes oneself into a small corner of the romance one imagines. Freedom from the writer will be forged Houdini-like from the series of chains he invents for his act of prestidigitation.

II.

DEMON NUMBER
Damon and the Dice

Most American writers have to come to terms at some point in their career with sports, and Coover more persistently, perhaps, than most. His first novel, *The Origin of the Brunists*, is threaded by an abortive basketball game and the playing career of its narrator; "Gloomy Gus" is a football player's story; and in a collection that featured Donald Barthelme on baseball and Daniel Halpern on boxing, Coover wrote "Soccer as an Existential Sacrament" (it is a sort of survivor of a hundred-page account of the 1982 World Cup games in Spain, a piece preposterously long for the source of its commission in a slick magazine).[1] But if soccer has become a late passion, Coover knows that baseball is America's religion, and that it is so because it is America's special reaction to its own wildness, dream (or nightmare) of a lack of limits: It is the play that can be reduced to number. Or almost so. *The Universal Baseball Association, Inc., J. Henry Waugh, Prop.* is a meditation upon this paradox.

J. Henry Waugh, a fifty-six-year-old bachelor and petty accountant has invented a baseball game played with dice and charts, a double metonymy, a game substituted for a game. He is a genius at games, a mathematical genius who once invented "Intermonop," "a variation on Monopoly, using twelve, sixteen, or twenty-four boards at once and an unlimited number of players, which opened up the possibility of wars run by industrial giants with investments on several boards at once . . . strikes and rebellions by the slumdwellers between 'Go' and 'Jail'" (*UBA*, 44). But his game-playing originated in and ultimately returned to baseball. For a short time in his life he had

---

1. "Soccer as an Existential Sacrament," *Close-Up* 15, no. 1 (Winter 1985): 78–91.

gone to the ball park: "The first game I saw . . . the league's best pitcher that year threw a three-hit shutout. His own team got only four hits, but three were in one inning, and they won, 2–0. Fantastic game, and I nearly fell asleep . . . at home I would pick up my scoreboard. Suddenly, what was dead had life, what was wearisome became stirring, . . . unbelievably real . . . I found out the score-cards were enough. I didn't need the games" (166). This "reality" is "the records, the statistics, the peculiar balances between individual and team . . . no other activity in the world had so precise and com-prehensive a history" (49). And, as Henry remarks to his one friend, Lou Engel, "History. Amazing, how we love it. And . . . without numbers or measurements, there probably wouldn't be any history" (49). "Reality" is defined, rationalized, indeed, created by a history that is number. And in its "game" aspect, that is, the superimposition of limit by rule, reality is controlled by number. An accountant is the precisely correct metaphor for a Platonic God who made the world by weight and measure.

But number has another side, mysterious, a pattern beyond the pattern, a will to its own symmetries for which there is no rational accounting. As one player in the Association says: "Numerology. Lot of revealing work in that field lately" (219). And Henry marvels at length about the unconscious but compelling patterns that make it impossible to alter the structure of his league: "Seven — the number of opponents each team now had — was central to baseball. Of course, nine, as the square of three, was also important: nine in-nings, nine players, three strikes and four balls . . . four bases" (206).[2]

This doubleness of number is reflected in baseball's own double-ness. If it epitomizes statistical balance and comprehensive history, the ultimate rationality of codification, baseball paradoxically "at the same time" involves, as Henry says, "so much ultimate mystery" (45). It was this something discernible yet inscrutable, which Henry felt when he was attending ball parks: "I felt like I was part of

2. Coover's *Origin of the Brunists* is an exercise in inducing the reader to try to unravel an ultimately misleading complex of numerological signals and portents in mimesis of the numerological madness of the mystic sectarians within the novel. In *Pricksongs & Descants*, the Pauline victim of "A Pedestrian Accident" spends his dy-ing minutes working at the false puzzle of Kll, seen on a partially concealed truck that had struck him down; and the protagonist of "The Elevator" is obsessed by ver-sions of meaning on the fourteenth floor.

something there, you know, like in church, except it was more real than any church . . . for a while I even had the funny idea that ball stadiums and not European churches were the real American holy places. Formulas for energy configurations where city boys came to see their country origins dramatized, some old lost fabric of unity" (166).

The double realization of baseball as game and as mystery rite lies behind a remark by Henry that lies behind the complicated allegories that begin with the forgivable puns in the novel's title, concluding that the "prop" of the university is JHW: "Everywhere he looked he saw names. His head was full of them. Bus stop. Whistlestop. Whistlestop Busby, second base . . . Henry was always careful about names, for they were what gave the league its sense of fulfilment . . . the dice and charts . . . were only the mechanics of the drama, not the drama itself." Like Adam, like his own prototype Jehovah, he knows that "the basic stuff is already there. In the name. Or rather: in the naming" (46–48).

Let us look at the names, then, in the several "eras" of the novel, the "realities" that mediate, repeat, absorb one another. First, there is what can be labeled the "continuous era," in which J. Henry Waugh is an accountant. "Continuous," because in it Henry's employer is the German Zifferblatt ("clock dial"), the personification of "Ziffer" ("number") and its application to time. In this era Henry watches Zifferblatt and his clock, hastens out from work early, arrives late. He has lost all interest in his job, makes accounting blunders with ledger entries (which terrify him only because he might tragically miscalculate something in the annals of his baseball league), and plays a self-invented horse-race game surreptitiously at his desk. He talks to himself, drinks far into the night, rushes home to the baseball game on his kitchen table, and generally worries his fat, shy fellow-accountant Lou Engel, whom, in this Germanic context, one must presumably translate "Lucifer Angel." When he leaves the universe on his kitchen table, it is to abandon pastrami and beer and the labor of the game for brandy at Pete's Bar (where Pete has been renamed Jake because Henry recognized in him Jake Bradley, retired second baseman of the Pastimers [8]). Here he has a hearty friendship with a saggily aging B-girl, Hettie Irden — presumably Gea-Tellus, the earth mother ("she's everybody's type" [169]). Once Henry brings the celibate Lou to Pete's and offers to fix him up with Hettie, but in the end himself takes her home. Once also he makes the great decision to share his secret game with Lou, but the latter's misunderstanding of the spirit of probability and reality, plus his spastic clumsiness, almost wrecks the Association, and Henry drives him out of his life and restores order — but only at the point where he must institute ritual in place of game. In this era it seems clear that Jehovah offers participation to Lucifer, wrests from him the woman in the duel for the earth, repairs the ruins of his universe inflicted by Satan (by the sacrificial death of a player preposterously named to combine the baseball and fertility and Christian myths, Jock Casey).

But in this era, too, the allegory presses least upon our attention, its obviousness buried in the comic actions and reactions of J. Henry Waugh, picaresque accountant. Let us remember truisms for a moment to explain and place the function of the comic absurd in *The Universal Baseball Association, Inc.*

"What terrible game will you play with us?" asks the narrator at the close of "The Leper's Helix." But he has surely learned in the brief but total revisions of his role that game is the opposite of play. Game implies an "end," a victory sought as the result of obeyed formulae with all of the statistics that Henry leans upon, the prop's props. Play is endless because pointless, mimesis of or escape from the unpredictable openness of casuality. Plays are defined formally as unexpectedness: The "peripeteia," the untangling of comic and tragic patterns is, however often repeated, a recipe for the incalculable. There are so statistics for drama or child's play. Play denies the otherness even of that which it may mimic: There are no body counts at cowboys and Indians, no sickness in playing doctor, no funeral or finality at the end of *Lear*. We are gamesters and game, hunters and hunted, and as such we are deprived of that make-believe trying on of selves, masks, new starts that constitute the freedom of play. Even our freedom to make up the rules of the game turns into another measure of containment. These are the polarities between which Coover's creatures struggle toward definition or — that favorite word — fulfilment.

When he goes to Pete's (Jake's — old "Pastimer" he) Bar to relax from his game or to celebrate its triumphs, Henry is playful. He has imposed not only upon Pete but also upon Hettie and himself the names and images of his game. But he goes there as a "player" in every sense. And the players, unlike the statistics, the games, are names. Adopting the name of his favorite, an improbably successful rookie pitcher, letting that projected personality reproject into his own, Henry the aging recluse has a lavishly successful night of sexual play with Hettie.

"The greatest pitcher in the history of baseball," he whispered. "Call me . . . Damon."

"Damon," she whispered, unbuckling his pants . . . unzipping his fly . . . "Play ball" cried the umpire. And the catcher, stripped of mask and guard, revealed as the pitcher Damon Rutherford, whipped the uniform off the first lady ballplayer in Association history . . . then . . . they . . . pounded into first, slid into second heels high, somersaulted over third, shot home standing up, then into the box once more, . . . and "Damon!" she cried, and "Damon!" (29)

Nothing could seem more mediated, and yet this is one of two unmediated moments in the novel. Coover here permits the Germanic allegory of the continuous (and comic) era, to accept and to absorb into its sex play the metonymic baseball metaphor of the game. "Irden," Gea-Tellus, "had invented her own magic version, stretching out as the field, left hand as first base" (206). When Hettie and Henry play ball it is to accept the metaphor of baseball, that merely "mythic or historical form" that Coover's "prólogo" said literature must simultaneously build upon and transcend. Learning Henry's mythic game vocabulary, she absorbs its geometrical limits into the unlimited world of play, offers him the recognition that the magic in names, words, is their limitless possibilities (was he not, after all, the one who "everywhere he looked . . . saw names"?) for freedom from any source they may have had: "I got it, Henry, I got it! come on! come on! keep it up! Behind his butt she clapped her cold soles to cheer him on . . . And here he comes . . . he's bolting for home, spurting past, sliding in — pow! . . . Oh, that's a game, Henry! That's really a great old game!" (34–35).

But the allegory turns upon its source. On the night before introducing Lou to his Association, Henry has his second bout with Hettie, this time in the role of another player, Damon's rival, the veteran pitcher Swanee Law. As they leave the bar to go home, he thinks, "Earthy . . . Won't be the same, he realized. No magic" (170). And the following morning he is edging dangerously close to a fatal, Quijote-like awakening:

Not once, in the Universal Baseball Association's fifty-six long seasons of play, had its proprietor plunged so close to self-disgust, felt so much like giving it up, . . . an old man playing with a child's toy; he felt somehow like an adolescent caught masturbating. (171)

With this mood upon Henry, Hettie discovers the imaginary nature of his enterprise, and it is with total silence that he rejects her humane understanding as she tries to reassure him of her affection. "Suddenly, astonishingly, she burst into tears. 'Ah, go to hell, you loony bastard!' . . . He heard her heels smacking down the wooden stairs and . . . out into the world" (175). That same night Lou Engel physically and psychically all but destroys the Association, and Henry sends him out of his haven into hell with the appropriate curse: "You clumsy goddamn idiot!" Lou's last communication is a call from the office to inform Henry of his dismissal by Zifferblatt, a call highlighted by the final anguished and outraged cry of Zifferblatt, which sums up his, ours, and Henry's own attitude toward the strange conduct of J. Henry Waugh: "(WHAT THE HELL DOES THIS MEAN — !!)" (210). And, finally, on this same tragic day the dice decree the death of the veteran Jake Bradley, Pete's player counterpart, so that Pete's Bar, too, must be given up forever.

Without the spirit of unmediated play which was only once possible in that magic night game between Hettie and Henry-cum-Damon, the old Pastimer's paradisal bar has no further function. All is gone, all lost now.

In the original days of the Association there began a breakdown into two political parties interested in capturing the chancellorship in the Association elections held every four years. One was the Bogglers, individualists led by the original chancellor, Barnaby North. The other was the Legalists, the party of Swanee Law, the star pitcher whom Damon Rutherford was about to transcend at his tragic death. Play is over, as Henry looks upon play, upon playing with oneself, as disgusting. J. Henry Waugh has joined the Legalists, as his assumption of Law's persona for his love games told us. He is an angry God of the Old Testament whose Pyrrhic victory now reverses the apparent reading of the German allegory. Hettie goes, like Eve, exiled out into the world of time; the world in which Lou the clumsy angel works for old clock face, Zifferblatt. And with Lou's call, Jehovah is exiled from that world, our world, into the solipsism imaged by his masturbating simile. Hettie's parting words ring prophetic: "Ah, go to hell, you loony bastard!" He did, by staying home. This is the novel's first version of, to borrow a phrase, the disappearance of God.

But with the world in shambles it does not end. And here begins the second and more complicated era of allegories: the era in which J. Henry Waugh is Proprietor of, and in closest touch with, the Universal Baseball Association. It is the "new Rutherford era" (31), exciting and yet somehow melancholy. "Maybe it was only because this was Year LVI: he and the Association were the same age, though, of course, their 'years' were reckoned differently. He saw two time lines crossing in space at a point marked '56.' Was it the vital moment?" (50). Numbers are having their mystic way again, to remind us that there are within Henry's Association the double aspect of rationalized history and of "utlimate mystery," which Henry found in baseball itself, mysteries ultimately hidden even from the Proprietor.

Let us recall the history of the Association. Under Barnaby North's chancellorship, the first truly great crop of rookies came up in Year XIX, the greatest being the Pioneers' pitcher Brock Rutherford; indeed, the glorious XXs became known as "the Brock Rutherford era" (22). Now Brock, also fifty-six-years-old in Year LVI, had sired a second son (an earlier one only partially successful), Damon, the magic pitcher who might transcend the father, who pitches a perfect game, who overshadows veteran ace Swanee Law. But as Damon is pitching on Henry's complex Extraordinary Occurrences Chart a three-dice throw shows 1–1–1: "Batter struck fatally by beanball." The pitcher, innocent of intent, was the Knickerbockers' Jock Casey. Brock's former teammate Barney Bancroft, now manager of the Pioneers, and so of the fated Damon, carries on the season; so does J. Henry Waugh.

When Lou Engel is permitted to become the only other ever to share in Henry's game, it is at a point in the season when Jock Casey is once again to pitch against the Pioneers. Lou plays to win, and he wins against all logic, all averages, wildly. Henry has been playing the season through since Damon's death without keeping records, throwing and throwing the dice. He has lost imaginative contact with his players (but this is the first instance in which the contact is lost not by Henry's disengagement, but by that of his creatures): "It was strangely as though they were running from him afraid of his plan, seeing it for what it was: the stupid mania of a sentimental old fool" (176). The "plan" becomes clear when Lou's rolls of the dice suddenly bring Jock Casey the killer into jeopardy upon the Extraordinary Occurrences Chart. Henry tenses in anticipation of order, throws the retributional dice, and sees "2-6-6, a lot less than he'd hoped for" (198). At this moment Lou spills beer over the Association records and is cast out. After Lou's departure, Henry stands in terror at his crossroads: "Damon Rutherford . . . it was just a little too much, and it wrecked the whole league . . . He smiled wryly, savoring the irony of it. Might save the game at that. How would they see it? Pretty peculiar. He trembles . . . Now, stop and think, he cautioned himself. Do you really want to save it? . . . Yes, if you killed that boy out there, then you couldn't quit, could you? No, that's a real commitment, you'd be hung up for good, they wouldn't let you go" (200–201). Casey stands ready to pitch: "Why waiting? Patient . . . Enduring . . . Casey played the game, heart and soul. Played it like nobody had ever played it before" (201). Waiting Casey stands "alone": "Sometimes Casey glanced up at him — only a glance, split-second pain, a pleading" (202). St. Mark reminds us that "at the ninth hour Jesus cried . . . My God, my God, why hast thou forsaken me?" And then the agony is over. Henry picks up the dice: "'I'm sorry, boy,' he whispered, and then . . . he set them down carefully . . . One by one. Six. Six . . . Six" (202). The number of the beast: pitcher killed by line drive.

One allegory cries out for attention. UBA, USA. Rutherford for Ruth, certainly, but also for rue. The Rutherfords, leaders of the Pioneers (read New Frontier) are special: "Maybe it was just the name that had ennobled them, for in a way . . . they were . . . the association's first real aristocrats" (12). The Kennedy myth of national renewal aborted is reflected in a series of killings following upon Henry's assassination of Jock after the death of Damon. Barney Bancroft — the latter-day echo of Barnaby North — eventually becomes chancellor and is assassinated, bringing on a revolt of the Universalists (220). The chancellor in Year LVI is, like Henry, a Legalist, and like LBJ, a paradox: "He looked old-fashioned, but he had an abiding passion for innovation. He was the most restless activist ever to take office . . . He was coldly calculating, yet supremely loyal to old comrades" (147). And when the season continues in an unprecedentedly gloomy and unpopular course, like Henry he must say: "And there's not a goddamn thing I can do about it" (150). His heir and alter ego is that grand southerner Swanee Law. Again, allegory by metonymy. We are directed to read through the layer of the accountant Jehovah to the history of the USA in the sixties, to see the sacrifice of Casey, the consequent helpless commitment of Henry and the chancellor as Vietnam, to hear the surge of revolution rolling in from the future. Politics and war are, after all, the great American games.

But if Swanee Law, in his symbiotic relationship with the current Legalist chancellor, focuses analogy upon LBJ, he can show us an even darker layer of the allegorical palimpsest. Nothing will come of nothing. The mystery of history is the regress of its sources, each carefully measured effect having its cause until we arrive at the Zenonian paradox inverted, infinity the ineffable first cause. "To be good," Henry once thought, "a chess player, too, had to convert his field to the entire universe, himself the ruler of that private enclosure — though from a pawn's-eye view, of course, it wasn't an enclosure at all, but, infinitely, all there was" (156). Theologically, it is safest to assume that the first cause is the will of God; as the chess passage suggests, associationalogically it seems safe to assume that the first cause is the will of J. Henry Waugh. There it began, properly, precisely, in Year 1. Or did it? Does that "beginning" only raise the question of inscrutability again, hint at another history, a mirror-corridor in which JHW is only some middle term? The question worries him: "The abrupt beginning had its disadvantages. It was, in a sense, too arbitrary, too inexplicable. In spite of the . . . warmth he felt toward those first ballplayers, it always troubled him that their life histories were so unavailable to him: what had a great player already in his thirties been doing for the previous ten years?" (45). Nothing can come of nothing. "It was, in fact, when the last Year 1 player had retired that Henry felt the Association had come of age, and when, a couple of years ago, the last veteran of Year 1, old ex-chancellor Barnaby North, had died, he had felt an odd sense of relief: the touch with the deep past was now purely 'historic,' its ambiguity only natural" (46).

"The basic stuff is already there. In the name." What then of the name, the, to Henry, always ambiguous nature, of Barnaby North, first chancellor and so first projection of the Proprietor himself within the Association; or, if JHW is only a middle term, perhaps the prototype of the prop himself? What this name tells us in conjunction with the rise of Swanee Law is that the Association's history has moved from North to South, a steady fall on any map.

The major portion of Coover's novel takes place in the critical Year LVI, the "new Rutherford era" in the Association. And the allegory is obviously written over the New Testament. It confuses because Damon Rutherford is so clearly the life-bringer; Jock Casey, his killer, is so clearly the Christ. But it is nonetheless obviously written over the new Testament, in which Matthew told of the Wise Men "saying . . . we have seen his star in the east, and are come to worship him" (Matt. 2:2). And it is in this sacred geography that one can place Henry's baserunner: "Out of the east, into the north, push out to the west, then march through the south back home again; like a baserunner on the paths, alone in a hostile cosmos, the stars out there in their places, . . . he interposed himself heroically to defy the holy condition . . . not knowing his defiance was merely a part of it" (141).

The sun rises in the East; as runner he moves at once toward the North. Lucifer, too, who said in his heart, "I will exalt my throne above the stars of God [Swanee Law is a Star, Damon only a Rookie]: I will sit also upon the mount of the congregation, in the sides of the north . . . I will be like the Most High" (Isa. 14:13–14). Is *he*, Barnaby North, original or image of the creator of the Universal Baseball Association? Or neither? Is he the founder because (infinite inscrutability of beginnings, or, mystery that denies beginnings) he is not the father but the son (remembering that, should this be so, the paradox is enacted twice over. Barney Bancroft, the Pioneer manager and future chancellor, being his namesake, whose assassination set off the revolution). So he seems when we recall, from the Acts of the Apostles, "Barnabas (which is being interpreted, the son of consolation)" (4:36).

Scripture speaks parables against the South (Ezek. 20:45–49), as does American politics, but we must return to the basic metaphors. Like JHW, the southerner is Law — the law of averages, the opposite of Damon Rutherford who breaks them. "Law knew what he had going for himself: whenever sportswriters interviewed him, they were shown large charts he kept tacked to his wall, indicating his own game-by-game progress . . . ['Pappy'] Rooney [his manager] had to laugh at Law's prostrating himself before the dirty feet of history" (145). Swanee Law the Legalist set against Barney Bancroft and his prototype, Barnaby North, founder of the opposed free party. The rationalization of history, number, the averages are where Henry, Jehovah, and the Association seem to be going, and we remember that it was Swanee who replaced Damon so tragically in Hettie's favors.[3] But there is a countercurrent within the Association as there is within J. Henry Waugh. Damon Rutherford the son is dead, but Barney Bancroft — manager, elder father figure to Damon but nominally son to Barnaby North, the child (and yet the mysterious elder) of J. Henry Waugh — knows the limits of Henry's and Swanee Law's history. "Bancroft, the rationalist, disbelieved in reason. It was the beast's son, after all, not the father, and if it had a way of sometimes getting out of hand, there was always limits . . . Re: back again, the primitive condition, the nonreflective operating thing: res. His son" (95).

When Damon was struck down, "the Proprietor of the Universal Baseball Association . . . brought utterly to grief, buried his face in the heap of papers on his kitchen table and cried for long bad time" (76). Well he might, victim of his own laws: "Even though he'd set his own rules, . . . and though he could change whenever he wished, nevertheless he and his players were committed to the turns of the mindless and unpredictable — one might even say, irresponsible — dice" (40). When Damon's fate is rolled, the players press around him crying "Do something! But do what? The dice were rolled" (73). And yet, after this time of weeping Henry goes out into the accountant's world, and he carries into it his sense of deity: "Feeling sour. Undiscoverable sun at four o'clock in the hazy sky. But a kind of glow in the streets, mocking him. Later, he'd have it rain" (77). God has not disappeared. He is a loony bastard, who thinks he controls the universe. But he has become mad because he has become a Legalist, lost contact with Barney Bancroft's, Barnaby North's boggling world, forgotten the paradox that he once had been able to apply to chess: "Henry enjoyed chess, but found it finally too Euclidean, too militant, ultimately irrational." Chess is game without the magic,

---

3. Swanee is verbally paralleled to Henry at the appropriate point: "Power and control. In and out. The old eagle, Swanee Law, just reared back and burned them in" (144). After the death of the sexually magic Damon, when Henry, in the adopted role of Swanee, prepares for his second sex game with Hettie, "Won't be the same, he realized. No magic . . . In and out, high and low. Just rear back and burn it in" (170).

without play; he found it, "in spite of its precision, formless really – nameless motion" (156).

Names not numbers are the drama, that which defies the predestinarian, "irresponsible" dice to turn formulaic number into mythic formulae. That is what happened to the Universal Baseball Association when JHW did something about it and tipped the die that killed Casey. The consequences were cosmic: He ceased to have connection with Hettie, Lou, Zifferblatt, but with his commitment he paradoxically also ceased to have conjunction with his players.

Here we must notice a principal narrative technique: After Damon's death, while Henry is gradually withdrawing himself from his accountant's world, he inversely projects himself into the players to the extent that the interior monologue of Henry, which seems the chief device of the earlier sections as he imagines activities in his Association, becomes a series of interior monologues on the part of individual players through which Henry's direct persona emerges less and less often until the day with Lou and Hettie, when he surfaces to almost give up his universe.

Yet one important example of Henry's absorption into his players both bears out and immensely modifies this general truth. It demonstrates Coover's technique of creating unbroken chains of interillumination between Henry's life world and his created universe. And it does so at the crucial point of choice, the point at which Damon dead, he can go on by the rules, quit the game, or sacrifice Jock Casey.

Henry, sleepless and broken by the death, visits the puzzled Lou's apartment (unable to be alone) to "imagine"/attend Damon's funeral. He seeks out a recording of Mozart's *Archduke*, drinks; the alarmed friend listens to his jumbled talk, assuming, of course, that the death has been that of a close friend. His innocent question, "Did he leave any . . . family?" gives Henry the first suggestion for how he could continue: To himself he muses "A son? Yes, he could have, he could have at that, and his name . . . ?" (88). There is nothing in the previous image, imagings of Damon, of this golden child athlete, young hero, to make such a history probable, and Henry realizes it implicitly in his next move; fleeing Lou's apartment for Jake's Bar, he creates a wake, a death-drunk of all the Old Timers reflecting his own manic grief. Before it begins, he accounts for all who are *not* in attendance, including Damon's older brother, a failed second-class player from a few seasons earlier. But he *had* been a ballplayer, had his moment of history with the league, and bore the magic name. So Henry imagines through him a more plausible, if indirect route to continuities:

He'd bolted for home the minute the burial was over, dragging his missus behind him, and there, pressed by an inexplicable urgency, had heisted her black skirts, and without even taking time to drop his pants, had shot her full of seed: yes, caught it! she said, and even he felt that germ strike home. (93)

They were right. Later, horny and half-drunk in a restaurant, Henry gazes on a waitress, a young frump, and thinks about her as the possible mother of this new potential: "Young Brock was handsome, elegant in his way, but it was easy to see that in a real ball game he just didn't have it. Something vital was missing. How would this son — Henry assumed it would be a boy — turn out? . . . Might be worth twenty more seasons just to find out" (159–60). But clearly his heart was not in it, for Henry has already remade an improbable history on the little cue offered by Lou's innocent query.

Probably the oldest and most cynical of Henry's avatars among the Old Timers who gather for the wake at Jake's is Rags Rooney, whose idea it had been. Sycamore Flynn, the manager of the pitcher who had killed Damon, attends but leaves very early, and Rooney laments that "Sick Flynn was gone, he'd had a few more things he'd like to jab him with. Like shotgunning poor Damon for jumping his virgin daughter" (110). While the wake is in progress, but before this remark, Hettie, unaware of the imaginary crowd at Jake's, approaches Henry in hopes of another great old game pitched at her by Damon:

He hadn't noticed her there before. She winked cheaply and asked: "How's Damon's pitching arm tonight?"
"He's dead."
"Hunh?"
"Damon Rutherford is dead."
It was as though he'd struck her in the face . . . When he looked up again, she was gone. (98)[4]

---

4. She does not go far from Henry's imagination, though. Later he fantasizes her having a gangbang with *all* the players at the wake, a little reflex thought, perhaps, of a different sort of son, as "they seeded her well, they stuffed her so full . . . it was a goddamn inundation" (115).

The incident merges with a reaction the others have to Sycamore
Flynn, himself merging with Henry: "It was funny abou Sic'em: they
all loved the bastard, pure gold the man's heart, yet this night they
couldn't get close to him. Wasn't his fault. Yet something was happening" (94). Then Flynn emerges *from* Henry, having left the bar.
He is on a train, "his mind in trouble pitched here and there, rocked
by the wheels' pa-clockety-knock, jogged loose from the continuum . . . the sons and the fathers, the sons and the fathers" (116).[5]
There are three rationales for Flynn's parental concern. One is his
emergence from Henry. A second is his long rivalry through his
stellar playing years with Damon's father, Brock Rutherford. The
two greats of their era, now known as the Brock Rutherford Era:
"Brock the Great. Oh yes, damn it, damn him, he was?" (118). The
last is his own paternity, the guilt and the loss when his daughter,
too, accepts some version (before or after the act) of Rooney's barb
about Flynn having killed Damon out of a father's jealousy. When he
killed Damon as her Daemon lover before Hettie's face in Jake's, she
had fled Henry. Now we learn the name of Flynn's daughter, fled like
Hettie from the man who robbed her of Damon's young sexuality
once, maybe twice:

His daughter had disappeared. She'd left no note. Hadn't been necessary. He
knew what she was telling him and there was nothing he could do about it,
nothing he could do that would bring her back. Harriet was as dead to him
now as her Damon was to Brock. Even more so, because Damon died and
left no hate behind. In a way, Flynn envied Brock. No, that wasn't true.
You're just trying to smooth it over, ease the guilt. (117)

It is an immense inner narrative developed in a few strokes by
Henry's imagination. This is not surprising, in any of its aspects but
one. He has been working fast with the idea of Damon having an
heir; he has dismissed Henrietta by discarding his Damon avatar
brutally, as Flynn has lost Harriet. But Flynn *is* Henry's alter ago,
and so neither intentionally beaned Damon — that was the mindless-

5. This is not random, but a portmanteau of all Henry's concerns: pa/father;
clock/Zifferblatt; knock/the beaning. If this strikes the reader as my critical free
association, one might remember Coover's own comment on Damon's funeral in
relation to his reading in preparation for the novel: "I . . . found a lot of good
Aramaic and Hebrew words I was able to make puns of; for example: the words for
'confusion' and 'emptiness,' *tohu* and *bohu*, enter . . . where Rooney is leading the
mourners to Purcell's music and they're going, 'Tee hee hee hee hee hee, boo hoo
hoo hoo' . . . I don't anticipate people seeing these things" (*First Person*, 149).

ness of the dice. What then, and it is crucial at this juncture, is Flynn's "guilt"?

He descends from the train near the ball park, a short walk to his hotel, and enters us into one of the most successful and eerie of those deliriums, which are not quite dreams, that punctuate Coover's work, but especially in the psychic life of Richard Nixon in *The Public Burning*.

It begins on this problem of "guilt." Flynn is in Damon's hometown; he might be recognized and harassed, so he walks, choosing "the dark streets. What was hounding him? That he didn't feel guilty *enough*?" (118). He passes the stadium, which "bulked, unlit in the dark night, like a massive ruin, exuding a black odor of death and corruption" (one remembers that Henry thinks that these now bare quires, "ball stadiums and not European churches were the real American holy places" [166]). But Flynn's experience goes beyond this: the Pioneers' Park has become unfamiliar. "No, no gates. Not even the hinges for one. And inside: it shouldn't be that black in there" (119). He feels about the walls of the suddenly unfamiliar passageways to the dugout, to the field. He discerns ghosts, he retreats, he finds himself disoriented. On the darkened ball field he feels the presence of all his players around him in the dark, Jock Casey, most poignantly, on the mound behind him. It is a ghost field because Casey is there: "'That you, Jock?' Turn around and look, you ass. Can't. Sorry, just can't . . . Flynn was near tears. Behind him, he realized, past Casey, past home plate, there was an exit. Maybe it was a way out, maybe it wasn't" (122–23).

Flynn has absorbed Henry, Henry's grief, taken Henry home into the old ball park of his lonely spooky apartment full of the deaths of all these paper heroes. "Maybe it was a way out, maybe it wasn't. But he'd never make it. He couldn't even turn around. And besides, he wasn't even sure what he'd find at home plate on the way. 'I quit,' he said. But then the lights came on" (123). In Henry's apartment. And when they did, he had given up the notion of quitting or continuing the Rutherford myth on the sheerness of chance of those dice, those numbers he had for so long thought of as order. Out of that dark dream, Henry had decided to intervene.

When young Damon is about to pitch in the fatal game succeeding his perfect performance, Henry's imagination works overtime: "'Go out and win one for the old man, son.' Who said that?

Why old Brock! Yes, there he was, sitting in a special box . . . In fact, Henry realized suddenly, 'it must be Brock Rutherford Day at Pioneer Park'" (64). That "it must be" takes on a redimensioning ambiguity analogous to the ambiguous status of Barnaby North, when, observing the wake for Damon, Henry's consciousness is expressed through that of successive participants in the festivities until it emerges as that of the chancellor: "Brock Rutherford Day had been Fenn's own idea. The whole UBA was suddenly bathed in light and excitement and enthusiasm. Fenn had foreseen an election sweep . . . The Guildsmen [at the time it was written read Goldwaterites] couldn't find a candidate. Total mandate. And then that pitch. He wasn't sure what he could do about it . . . The only conceivable forms of meaningful action at a time like this were all illegal" (104). But "illegality," breaking of the rules and the substitution of sacrifice for chance, commitment for causality, predestination for percentages — these are phrases to describe Henry's deliberate killing of Jock Casey with the number of the beast from the Book of Revelation: And we might here remind ourselves that Coover's "prólogo" speaks of fiction as the use of "familiar forms to combat the content of those forms, . . . to conduct the reader . . . away from magic to maturity, away from mystery to revelation." The mediation is so intensified that we are led to search for answers to impossible questions, those that haunt Henry's sense of history: Is the chancellor Henry's "persona," or Henry the chancellor's? A familiar gambit, echo of the doubleness of Barnaby North, of Montaigne's puzzle about his playful cat. Until we arrive at the mythic era with which the novel concludes, "Damonsday CLVII."

Now JHW is gone; this the second, the defining disappearance of the god of the game. The world has become a ritual because he sacrificed Jock Casey to save his universe, not man's. The Christian myth is reenacted as a myth of the Beast who is anti-Christ. In this era, "some writers even argue that Rutherford and Casey never existed — nothing more than another of the ancient myths of the sun, symbolized as a victim slaughtered by the monster or force of darkness" (223–24). The New Testament sources of Coover's allegories, like the Old Testament sources, are turned back upon themselves.

There is no narrative interaction now between Henry and his players — they have absorbed his consciousness both in narrative style and in literal fact: One player named Raspberry Schultz "has turned . . . to the folklore of game theory, and plays himself some device with dice" (234). J. Henry Waugh reduced to a Bronx cheer. He exists only in the tangled confusions of skepticism and ignorance with which the players attempt to understand the meaning of the political parties that in a ritual world have become theological sects, attempt to wring some meaning out of the annual reenactment of the game in which Damon Rutherford was killed, the games of "Damonsday."[6] The sun dominates the players and the imagery on this mythic day that closes the novel, and the old interaction between the two levels of phenomena mediated by Henry's consciousness is allowed to appear in reverse just once in a player's joke: "'Pull the switch on that thing, man!' Gringo hollers up to the sun . . . 'Yeah,' 'What does it say?' '100 Watt.'" (231–32). They are all gone as though they never existed: JHW, Rutherford, and Casey. Only Damon remains.

The cynical rookie chosen for the role resents and fears it, lives in a surrealistic shadowland where an apparitional boy demands an autograph, where women surround him and tear at his fly as he struggles through an Orphic threat. He reviews the theological debate upon the meaning of the Parable of the Duel, which is about to be reenacted and rejects it all, all but one thing: "Damon the man, legend or no" (221). "Just remember," he tells himself as he dresses for the Duel, "how you love the guy, that second son who pitched such great ball, and died so young" (223) (read JFK).

Dressed, he stands on the mound as Damon feeling the mark of the Beast. He "flexes his fist, staring curiously at it, . . . thinking he's got something special there today" (232), feeling that mark "in the right hand," as before and after "in the forehead" that is the Beast's (Rev. 13:6; 2:4). The doubter who must enact the catcher walks toward him. "He has read all he can find on the Association's history, and he knows he is nothing" (239); "His despair is too complex for plain speech . . . He is afraid. Not only of what he must do. But of everything" (238). "He stares at the sky, beyond which there is more sky, overwhelming in its enormity. He, . . . is utterly absorbed in it, entirely disappears, is nothing at all" (238).[7] Perhaps

---

6. Henry's sense of the religious function of baseball, first felt in the accountant's trip to the ballpark (166), has been fulfilled as the only residue of his game. Now, again, but in a new sense, he does not "need the games."

7. Mel Trench, his ancestor, lived with a constant sense of death (106–8).

Henry has heard Gringo's joking command and turned out the light over the table, for as the doubter contemplates his terror, he realizes that "it's coming, Yes, now, today, here in the blackening sun" (241). And then he arrives at the mound. It is the second unmediated moment in the novel. He confronts Damon and sees that "it's all there is." And Damon sees, too, but inverts the sense of the vision. The joke of the 100-watt sun echoes an image from Henry's consciousness at the very beginning, when he realizes that sometimes his game is just dead statistics to him, no names: "just a distant echo . . . But then . . . someone like Damon Rutherford came along to flip the switch, turn things on" (14). Damon sees, and gives light and life again: "He says: 'Hey, wait, buddy! You love this game, don't you?' . . . Damon grins. Lights up the whole goddamn world. 'Then don't be afraid' . . . he says. And the black clouds break up, . . . and his [Trench's, the battery mate's] own oppressed heart leaps alive to give it one last try." " 'It's not a trial,' says Damon, glove tucked in his armpit, hands working the new ball . . . 'It's not even a lesson. It's just what it is.' Damon holds the baseball up between them. It is hard and white and alive in the sun" (242).

Two young friends together in a numerical, Platonic world that defies cynicism. Damon, the Pythagorean who offered himself for Pithias in the name of friendship to save them both by love. To save them from death imposed by a tyrant.

Paul Trench's unmediated moment of life, like Henry's, is given through Damon. Both are moments in which the tyranny of game is converted into the improbability of play: "You love this game," he affirms for Trench; "That's really a great old game," affirms Hettie. The relationship of J. Henry Waugh and Jock Casey, Coover's God and Jesus Christ, had inverted the Christian myth upon which it was founded. But the third person of Coover's trinity rights it again, or rather rewrites it, with the central holy pun. J. Henry Waugh is inspired, as is his Association, by the presence of Damon, that holy name whose Greek original meant not only the inevitable divine power mediating between gods and men but also those souls of the dead whom we honor, especially, explains the OED, "deified heroes." As Henry said, "The basic stuff is already there. In the name. Or rather: in the naming." By naming, Coover converts the dark parable of our insane culture into an affirmation that salvation is still possible through that daemonic sense of play with which we are so richly endowed.

Let us now reconsider *The Universal Baseball Association, Inc.* (for that is what it is, Lou's flood of beer and Henry's rainbow wiping out the carefully penned boxscores and histories of a world gone wrong) under a different rubric; let us consider it as a sophisticated metafiction, a novel in the tradition of writings about writings. It has been examined in this context, and it is reasonable that it should be. It narrates a history perfectly separated from the ambiguities and impossibilities that separate the historical, even the least historical, novel — one mimetic only of a generalized place, time, space — from the text. Because here the history is of a text, a history that claims existence only in ink. A novel about a man, or a god, or a madman who substituted writing for life. And then, within that writing there were all those groups, the Bogglers and Legalists, conservatives and radicals, mythologists and rational demystifiers, who interpret the first seven chapters in the eighth. And we are left to play out our own critical fantasies in the missing ninth inning, chapter, life of the cat (is not Coover's story "The Cat in the Hat for President," like this novel, about a book that comes into independent life?). And none of this is true to our reading. John Barth's *Chimera* is about the telling of stories, about the impossibility of it. *The Universal Baseball Association, Inc.* is not. Or rather, it uses the notion of authorship and its authority to tell a story, a history, a *historia* just as the Quijote does. As the author of the association is drawn into his game of chance measured against balance (*is* the book we read, after all, perhaps Barney Bancroft's history of the *UBA in the Balance*?), we are drawn with him into the names, not the numbers. The argument of "writing" becomes the vehicle of a larger argument. In this larger argument, characters may argue the ontology of their self-existence, as did Raspberry Schultz, Paul Trench, and others on "Damonsday CLVII," but we do not argue their existence, we embrace it as the function of narrative. The writer's vehicle is always the reader's tenor: This collusion makes a story seem a history. And that is what makes the novel novel: It always purveys news of a new life.

But then there *are* writings that are not novel, that draw our attention in quite other directions, draw it into coactivity with the

author, the writer, who must restrain but also repeat genres. These
are almost inevitably shorter, because repetition cannot sustain itself
indefinitely.

There is, for instance, a story in *Pricksongs & Descants* about
reading. "The Marker" is about a bookmark. A man reads; his nude,
lovely wife prepares for bed. Stimulated (by the book, by the sight of
her?) he seeks her laughter in the dark. The room has changed, he
loses direction, fears, finds, and fucks her only to be broken in upon
by a police quintet as he discovers his wife to be a rotting corpse. His
genitals are shredded by the police; he is given a lecture on genre (he
earns it, having in the dark prediscovery of the palpable body rede-
fined his wife into "an abstract Beauty") by the officer who has been
thinking hard about the matter:

I am not, in the strictest sense, a traditionalist . . . I am personally con-
vinced . . . that innovations find their best soil in traditions, which are justified in their own turn by the innovations which created them. I believe, then,
that law and custom are essential, but that it is one's constant task to review
and revise them. (91)

This is Coover's self-parody of the dedicatory talk with Cervantes
about writing and revision, about genres. The reader/writer of this
fiction is trapped in banal tradition, immured much more deeply
("He stands, returns her gaze for almost a minute without smiling,
and then does smile, at the same time placing his book on the table"
[89]) than the policeman who, like Henry when his literary tradition
betrays him, knows that *"some things still make me puke"* (91). The
corpse is decaying, stinks, as the league had begun to for Henry after
the death of Damon. But here in Jason, husband of "The Marker,"
there is only the metaphor of the crushed genitals and the last cry as
he confuses the tenor and vehicle of a little parable about bad writing
and banal living: "The officer notices the book . . . flips through it
hastily . . . The marker falls to the floor. *'The marker!'* Jason gasps
desperately, but the police officer does not hear him, nor does he
want to" (92). Returns, repetitions, the generic are those things that
no one wants to hear. Unless one is in the mood to think of writing as
the imitation of repetition. And this ceases momentarily to bore only
in sex, or — verbalized — in pornography. There is a situational
kinetics built into Coover's large profile of pornography and the por-
nographer, that great moviemaker/aging star Lucky Pierre. His past

lies at his feet as abandoned women and film in "The Cunt Auction," as virgin memory in "Lucky Pierre and the Music Lesson." [8] But in *Spanking the Maid* (better titled in its original appearance in *Iowa Review* as "A Day's Work") there is nothing kinetic, only pornography simplified into its written essence as repetition. This is pleasure as boredom, a slow enactment of that self-conscious master-slave relationship that is the origin of all original and repetitive enterprises, stimulations. She is spanked, he is bored, needful; she is a grateful but bewildered tabula rasa. She discerns stories in the small histories of his sheets as she makes the bed. But discerns them badly, as he has failed to write them, or has written them badly. It is writing about repetition, about the maid and the master, but what is repeated is only the variation upon fantasy. One could apply the second epigraph in *Pricksongs & Descants*, that from Paul Valéry: "They therefore set me this problem of the equality of appearance and numbers." One could not apply the other epigraph, that from *Fanny Hill*: "He thrusts, she heaves."

The whole is a pastiche of nineteenth-century styles from the literature of pornography. The maid enters the room in the style he has taught her — "deliberately, gravely, without affectation, circumspect in her motions (as she has been taught)" (*SM*, 9). She errs in opening the window too abruptly to let "buckets" of light spill in, hearing the songs of birds (or not hearing them on occasion), throwing back the bed, cleaning the bathroom, and — always failing — raising her skirt and apron, lowering her drawers "as that seat chosen by Mother Nature for such interventions quivers and reddens under the whistling strokes of the birch rod in his hand" (41–42). It is an old story that draws them together in a generic enterprise ("Whish-SLASH . . . THWOCK!"). Like any reviser, editor, typesetter, generic epigone, the focus of her trouble is that she fails to get the sheets right, those sheets in which he has dreamed a recurrent dream that spawns the detritus of clues she fears finding every morning. He wakes to the days always older, trapped by the dream, expecting the day's punishment. If he could only be like her, seeking happiness in

8. Robert Coover and Larry McCaffrey, "Robert Coover on His Own and Other Fictions," in *Novel vs. Fiction: The Contemporary Reformation*, ed. Jackson I. Cope and Geoffrey Green (Norman, Okla., 1981), 62–63. "Lucky Pierre and the Music Lesson," *New American Review* 14 (New York, 1972), 201–12; "Lucky Pierre and the Cunt Auction," *Antaeus* 13–14 (Spring-Summer 1974): 155–61.

service to God and to him, anticipating the punishment that encour-
ages her to go on. He is, of course, the godlike writer. And she, her
buttocks, provide another sheet for the imprint of the text he so haz-
ily understands: "He often wonders, watching that broad part destined by Mother Nature for such solemnities quiver and redden
under his hand (he thinks of it as a blank ledger on which to write),
whether it is he who has given himself to a higher end, or that end
which has chosen and in effect captured him" (54).[9] For if he has, like
J. Henry Waugh, the godlike freedom to invent an absolute mastery
(What other genre is as kinetic as the written daydreams, nightmares
of sadomasochistic pornography?) over a world of blank ledgers, he
is directed by — precisely — genre:

Sometimes she must bend over a chair or the bed, or be horsed over the
pillows, the dresser or a stool, there are manuals for this. Likewise her
drawers: whether they are to be drawn tight over her buttocks like a second
skin or lowered, and if lowered, by which of them, how far, and so on. Her
responses are assumed in the texts . . . but not specified, except as they
determine his own reactions. (61)

But genres, like pornography, are simultaneously minutely in-
structive and frustrating in their distance from narrative, fact, the
novel, the new: The maid has been taught to repeat hymns on the
beauties of duty, hymns to a God they both must serve, the servants
of the servant of God. "But he, lacking superiors, must devote
himself to abstractions, never knowing when he has succeeded,
when he has failed, even if he has the abstractions right" (25). Each
asks when it all began, this sadomasochistic ritual: "When she
entered? Before that? Long ago?" (22); He does not know when,
where she entered, where she goes when the enactment is over. He,
she, weary with studying the problem of givens and change: "That
riddle of genesis . . . to wit, that a condition *has* no beginning. Only
change can begin or end" (23); "change . . . is eternal, has no beginning — only conditions can begin or end" (88); "What, is he snoring?
She . . . realizes with a faint shudder . . . that change and condition
are coeval and everlasting: a truth as hollow as the absence of bird-
song (but they are singing!)" (97).
   She, receptor, reader of that text written out of old *scenarii* on her

9. The maid enters late in the novella to change the bed "with stacks of crisp clean
sheets in her arms like empty ledgers" (91).

buttocks, knows that "something is missing . . . it's too repetitive" (28). That is the lesson of the master: "Arrangement and thought will give you method and habit" (37). But writing in the old vocabulary, limited by those manuals to the selection of instruments and positions, he too feels without purpose: "Every day the same. Why does he persist?" (53); she echoes the ennui of their fury: "She recites dutifully, but the words seem meaningless to her and go nowhere" (55). The whippings rise toward frenzy: "If improvisation is denied him, interpretation is not" (66–67). As he pushes the groupings of possibility to their limits, she recognizes his limits, the danger of escaping pattern: "If you don't stop . . . You — you won't know what to do *next!*" (77).

He takes stock of his instruments ("When the riddles and paradoxes of his calling overtake him, wrapping him in momentary darkness, he takes refuge in the purity of technique" [78]). But now all the old games, places, positions, words have been tried; if they have shared the myth of spiritual infusion through the anus with that asshole Nixon, it has failed "he thinks, staring gloomily at her soul's ingress which confronts him like blank paper" (81). But he labors on in the old formulae: "Watching the weals emerge from the blank page of her soul's ingress like secret writing, he finds himself searching it for something . . . dew-bejewelled hieroglyphics of crosshatched stripes. But no, the futility of his labors, that's all there is to read" (87). The writer caught in pornography, the generic metaphor for the self-abuse inherent in genres, has had a recurrent, if changing, dream throughout the course of his encounters with the abstract maid. The dream of writing is always new, but for the intimidated, always fugitive when set to words, as Coover's final metaphor implicitly laminates two asses, that of the maid, of course, with the master who has trapped them into mere exercises: "He can no longer remember, his mind is a blank sheet" (92).

This is an allegory about writing within genres, styles, limits. And in it Coover uses the least imaginative genre to force a sense of the final need for imaginative conquest of limits. It is much less mysterious than its French translator, Denis Roche, or the latest American cicerone through the corpus think.[10] It is about the stun-

10. See the miniessay on the back cover of Roche's translation, *La Bonne et son maître* (Paris, 1984), and Lois Gordon, *Robert Coover: The Universal Fictionmaking Process* (Carbondale, Ill., 1983), 163–66.

ning simplicity with which one can, with the manual of generic pre-
scription, proscription, with "method and habit," write oneself out of
"communication" with an audience, with one's own text, with one's
own self. *Spanking the Maid* is *about* this writers' problem because it
is not a pornographic, kinetic story. Jason had, at the least, a name,
before he turned his wife into abstract beauty and horror. Henry
knows that the naming is all, something quite beyond the method
and habit, the statistical markers by which baseball only approaches
the possibilities of art. But *The Universal Baseball Association, Inc.*,
in spite of, in defiance of, that title, is not about writing. It is written,
a history, notwithstanding that like most writing in the fictional
form, it is about people who do not live here. But, unlike the genre-
bound maid and her master, people who reenforce our desires while
living elsewhere.

The master and the maid, like all formulaists, do not help us imagine; they steal fantasies and then sterilize them. But Henry, like
Quijote, sacrifices himself to the strenuous powers of his imagination, as does any creator, to enlarge our own.

Between the extremes of Henry's wholly invented world and the
nearly historical world of *The Public Burning*, let us pause to consider the novel as genre or, possibly, as antigeneric in its nature.

III.

THE PUBLIC BURNING
Beyond the Dialogic Novel

It has been remarked from the earliest reviews that the Nixon of *The Public Burning* is a clown, but also one of the most humanized presentations of Nixon in fiction or in allegedly historical writing; certainly a more humanized figure than either Julius or Ethel Rosenberg, with whom Coover's instinctive political sympathies lay.[1] This was not so from the beginning of the projected novella that became this novel (Coover would have labeled it a "romance" had not the publishers demurred).[2] It was a long research job, nearly ten years in the making of its various stages. As the research grew, naturally Nixon grew in direct proportion; he is, after all, an immensely more complicated being than the Rosenbergs, and as they flattened into the roles they had chosen, Nixon expanded past any role. But this is a political novel, a historical novel with things to say about America, and Coover inevitably became nervous about the growth of Nixon past the limits characterizing the other pole of the "romance."

It was to exorcise this surprise and frustration that Coover wrote "Whatever Happened to Gloomy Gus of the Chicago Bears?" In the history of composition, this piece stands someplace past the middle of *The Public Burning* (thus claiming implicitly its parallelism to the "prólogo" of *Pricksongs & Descants*); in effect, though, it is prologue, and another metaphor about games, genres, and art. However, in its heavily revised form (rewritten a decade after the first version), it is also epilogue to the novel. And the revisions are worth careful study, because the first version was written in a rush of energy stimulated by Coover's desire to get to the end of *The Public*

1. See Coover's scathing review of Louis Nizer's *The Implosion Conspiracy* in the *New York Times Book Review*, 11 February 1973, 4–5.
2. *First Person*, 154.

Burning, whereas the second version is his contemplation on aesthetics, even on the urges that made the original novella necessary to the completion of *The Public Burning.*[3]

Let us summarize the story. It is 1936 in Chicago. The narrator, Meyer, is a sculptor in metal, specializing in athletes and acrobats.[4] He works for the Works Progress Administration, has learned his art by learning trades: wandering through the United States and the depression, he has worked at many, finally becoming a welder and, thus, metal artist. Meyer has become a careful and centerless miscellany of techniques — this is his rapport with that other student, Gloomy Gus. Meyer has also been radicalized politically, and he is in the throes of deciding whether he should join friends who have gone, or intend to go, to enlist in the Abraham Lincoln Brigade in the Spanish Civil War. Meyer's loft is a gathering point, and Mario is the labor strike organizer who is the most articulate and influential in the group. One evening the shooting star/star football player "Gloomy Gus" ("'Oh, Dick,'" his lover "groaned [she was the only one of us who ever used his real name]")[5] is introduced into this group. His career over, he has become "an actor in a WPA project" (50).

At first Gus's conduct is indecipherable; he reacts to his host's common courtesies with erotic responses. The entire party finds him in bed with an activist Jewish girl; he is oblivious to all courtesies. He is a case history for the leftist artist to learn: They both seem to have been born with two left feet (74) and the propensities for masking (Meyer is welding an enormous mask of Maxim Gorky, for which everything goes right but the eyes; Gus, at their first meeting, is characterized by "his eyes flicking from side to side as though deeply perplexed" [51]); self as mask, as the ever-potential possibility of becoming merely public, a name such as that the author, artist, politician puts at the foot of the caricature he has made: "Gloomy

3. Robert Coover and Larry McCaffrey, "Robert Coover on His Own and Other Fictions," in *Novel vs. Fiction: The Contemporary Reformation,* ed. Jackson I. Cope and Geoffrey Green (Norman, Okla., 1981), 59–60. Immediately following references are to the first version of the novella: "Whatever Happened to Gloomy Gus of the Chicago Bears?" *American Review* 22 (New York, 1975), 34–110.

4. Although he does not take into account "Gloomy Gus," any reading of *The Public Burning* in terms of performance and circus structure must be indebted to the insights of Thomas LeClair's "Robert Coover, *The Public Burning,* and the Art of Excess," *Critique* 23, no. 3 (1982): 5–28.

5. "I looked like a preacher the day I was born. Gloomy Gus, they called me" (Nixon in *PB,* 142).

Gus was the name that stuck to him . . . because it was a clown's name, and a clown was what Gus was, even when he was a National Hero" (42). That "even" tells us that Meyer knows about nature and roles: Gus was a born clown who had to intensify the role in acting it out to the bitter end (of *The Public Burning*). But roles are available only within contexts, and, within the theatricalized context that legitimizes one's self-presentation as clown, we have the circus, of course.[6] And that will come later. But there are a number of generic steps before Nixon comes naked upon the stage of Times Square.

Gus was a good boy with a bad family in Whittier, California. He was a debater, a scholarly student, a potential lawyer. He was also an uncoordinated athlete and lover — or would-be lover. But he was an actor in school plays, and it is his doing corny scenes from these plays that make his first visit to Meyer's loft memorable, and erotic. Meyer, pouring a drink, says "Tell me when." Gus replies with a shocker: "Honey, don't be impatient. The delay's been useful, hasn't it?" (51). Finally they grasp that he has a world of such lines from the forgotten plays upon which he has spun a self-characterization.

But the lines of the role cross over into another life; Gus has become the world's most effective lover. And before that, its greatest football player. It had all begun with that favorite game to which Richard Nixon had applied himself with determination but little success, as he had to dramatics. The Gus who should have become a lawyer, Coover's fantasy Nixon, was modeled upon one who failed on the football field but became a lawyer and all that led to. But here the role-playing is laid bare by a speeding up, as the football fantasy is allowed to become metaphor for the man who "had no core at all. Unless pure will-power had some kind of substance, amounted to some kind of character" (50–51).

Gus learns to play football, but is always offside. So he practices — nothing positive, just practices not being in such a hurry as to be offside. He times himself, and then times himself again in that other sport of love. The practice schedules become all-absorbing, he becomes all-American on the field and in bed, all-*pro*. The lawyer lost to the law: a professional without a vocation, just a schedule of

6. Cf. *First Person*, 155: "Originally, it was the circus aspect that interested me most," a comment about a time before Nixon entered Coover's conception as the central psyche of the enterprise.

moves. More and more intricate, more and more demanding moves: "learn one thing at a time, starting with the simplest, and practice it over and over and over until it was second nature (there being no first)" (80). The denouement is almost predictable. Gus had driven the Chicago Bears (Nikita Khrushchev and the Russians are always in the background [47], with an apolitical intent that can only be stressed by political pairings) to an undefeated championship season. But his playoff opponents learn that he *reacts* only to the numbers, they learn the magic number twenty-nine, which sets Gus into action (running offside, smashing his girlfriend when she mentions her age). His football career is finished, and he wanders into the radicals' circle.

Gus's death at a labor confrontation between strikers and strike-breakers opens the first layer of the novella's questioning. The Nixon of *The Public Burning* wants to understand. Gus has no such aspirations: "Gus not only lacked political awareness, he lacked awareness of any kind" (50); "It was this nothingness at the center that we all settled on as the essential Gloomy Gus" (51). So Gus dies, not as a rebel, an anarchist or organizer, but because he saw a gas grenade thrown and reacted as his football practice had taught him in running it for a touchdown ("He'd laid on several skills in his lifetime, and he didn't always come up with the right ones in the right order" [43]). The author trying to exorcise the increasingly human and therefore disturbing Nixon of the novel seems to do so in the novella when he sums up Gus: "He was a walking parody of Marx's definition of consciousness, a cartoon image of the Social Product, probably the only man in recent history with what could be called a naked superego" (65). But if he can pause, Coover cannot stop at caricature. Gus has a "bushy black beard," which makes one of the crowd recognize that "Goddamn! It's Karl Marx" (50). This is the cry that brings forth Meyer's denial that Gus had political consciousness. Perhaps. But who is that other bearded hero of a civil war before Spain's, namesake of "the Abraham Lincoln Brigade"; president of the United States, small-town lawyer, master of debate? The masks fall into unruly place ("I'd found a large picture of Abraham Lincoln and had pasted up a gigantic poster with a balloon coming out of Abe's mouth that read: VIVA LA QUINCE BRIGADA! . . . Mario laughed and called it jingoism" [50]). Marx and Lincoln and Gus and Gorky (at the first party Gus memorizes the words of "L'Internationale") — learning of Gus's death, Meyer thinks how "I might even be able to go back and weld another piece on Maxim Gorky's nose . . . His nose is broad and generous" (35). The company and comparisons are becoming mixed, and mixed in such unfinished combinations, over-lappings as to make political commitment as problematic as the cari-cature of Nixon as American hero, one who shared with Abraham Lincoln the fate of being zapped by Uncle Sam Slick into the presidency. Are they, then, separated by nothing more, in the end, perhaps, than generations? These are Coover's hovering jocoserious considerations. But Gus is a failure of self as politician because he is a triumph of bad art. He is generic man, parallel to the uncommitted artist Meyer.

Without politics, bonded by rules into minute-by-minute re-self-definitions, Gus is actor not author; but active and, had he known Meyer's lesson, perhaps also political, because, says the sculptor of athletes, "in football, as in politics, the issue is not ethical but aesthetic" (71). The artist begins to identify dangerously: "Both of us were ranging far from home, fulfilling myths about ourselves" (91); "When his moment came he gave — no explanations or advice — but himself. 'Like a poet'" (108). Art as unfinished process (Gorky's eyes), always projected but never performed (a theatrical metaphor that speaks to the confusion of the narrator). Meyer says of Gus that

one skill did not simply lead to another — more often it led to a dozen, and each of these dozen to a dozen each . . . I could understand his dilemma. I have the same problem with my sculpting . . . I'm afraid we had a lot in common, Gloomy Gus and I, . . . we simplified ourselves — but didn't we merely substitute a vertical madness for a horizontal one? (81)

It is, of course, Meyer's bad-faith rationalization for his failure to commit or complete his actions as anarchist or artist. He decides almost at the beginning against going to Spain in a pastoral dawn by the railroad tracks, where he gathers metal articles to be melded into his Gorky mask, an example of art as socialist realism. Or, art as im-itation (political portraiture, but needing the life of the eyes to make the mask meaningful). What had Meyer seen in Gus but an artist's excuse for dead art, for the frenzy of genres? A late scholar wrote a little book about the rage for order that drove artists of the Renaissance from the comfort of established genres to a mad proliferation of rules,[7] of genres mixed and made to fit every kind of imitation, to legitimize a self that Coover here calls "a naked superego." Gus's "thinking sessions were essentially efforts to crossbreed all the things he already knew, creating a greatly augmented number of variations on a theme . . . There were still patterns, . . . but they were much harder to detect and predict" (101).

But Meyer can see the genre-ridden protagonist (agonist) only in terms of games or sex. His confidante, Golda, who is Gus's lover, explains that "it's always the same, exactly the same" (58) And great; but why is she explaining, asking Meyer to watch for confirmation? Coover disposed of Nixon as a personality, and disposed of the monologic novel, a genre in which the author dominates voices if only by coordinating them; disposed of these things as best he could by writing the first version of "Gloomy Gus." But he did, of course, implicate himself, draw the author of the larger novelistic enterprise into his drawing off of tensions into this novella. It is about writing raised to a certain temperature, this divagation, that was coming too close to fusing author and stuff, artist and actor. So it became another piece of athleticism, another book like *The Origin of the Brunists* and *The Universal Baseball Association, Inc.*, about games. One that saved the real reserves for the contemplation of the possibility that politics might become a separate structure. And so Coover went on with *The Public Burning.*

The structures from *The Origin of the Brunists* and *The Universal Baseball Association, Inc.* are all here, the games and the numerology that accompanies them. Politics as a self-proliferation into athletics, sex, art. Hettie had almost made Henry stop counting when they copulated in the image of his own imagination. Gus dies by the numbers he had lived by; but the edging across the border into a creativity in both Hettie's case (not Henry's) and Gus's offers on the one hand a word about the limitations imposed, and, on the other, a way to look at Nixon's larger role in *The Public Burning.* Gus's was not a game or a party, or — as Damon said — even a lesson. He ran with the grenade with perfect timing through a crowd of opponents, "then turned back to walk toward the cops with his arms out-

7. Rosalie Colie, *The Resources of Kind: Genre-Theory in the Renaissance*, ed. Barbara K. Lewalski (Berkeley, 1973).

stretched [and] one of the cops shot him" (47). But unlike Damon, he had not learned the game: "He'd become like some terrifying symbol or something." Meyer doesn't want to believe this at a level deeper than the artist/athlete metaphor. But in a novella written during the composition of *The Public Burning*, it can scarcely be a coincidence that the otherwise minor character who has the insight into this symbol is named Sam: "If he's a bit berserk . . . he's only a mirror image of the insane nation that created him" (65).

Having totally worked out this metaphor in *The Public Burning*, Coover returned to "Whatever Happened to Gloomy Gus of the Chicago Bears?" and extended it into an independent work, a reconsideration of the whole complex relationship between himself, the developing Nixon of the developing novel, and the novella that we have just reviewed. And now new resonances dominate.[8]

There are small things, like the name Iron Butt, which Gus acquired as a football player, which occurs in identical phrasing in both versions, but has larger ironies after Nixon's inspiration by Uncle Sam at the close of *The Public Burning*: Randy in the first version, renamed Jessie in the second (we are into biblical naming) "speculated it had to do with his Bear teammates' inability to crack his virginity in the lockerrooms; he made up a funny song about it, a parody of 'John Henry' in which the steel-drivin' man meets his match at last" (43). Between the two tellings, Gus had accepted his homosexual fate as destiny's cruel love.

There are larger changes, too. Mario (one recalls all those Italian miners who represent the outrage of labor against the establishment in *The Origin of the Brunists*) becomes Leo, a Jew like Meyer whose involvement with Spain is only a station on his racial fantasy's journey to Palestine. Again, as in the early version, Meyer "followed them [Randy and Mario become Jesse and Leo] around in their efforts to organize coalminers, tenant farmers, ironworkers, housewreckers," but in the revision there is the added admission: "Leo becoming a kind of father-figure to me." Well he might. In the first version Meyer wanders through the depression as an American; in the revision, as a Jew. Following Leo as, perhaps, recovered *convertido* but certainly as a universal leader, the immancable lion who

8. Through Coover's generosity, I quote from a typescript novel not published as of this writing. An excerpt from this revised version of "Gloomy Gus" is, however, public: "That F'kucken Karl Marx," *Fiction International* 15, no. 2 (1984): 107–16.

returns in "Aesop's Forest": "Leo himself might once have been a Catholic for all we know, depending on whether his real name is Leopold, Leonardo, León, Leonid, or Leonides." All these wars and strike riots are a step toward the crucifixion that Nixon / Gus so symbolically embraced with the familiar V-sign that, absent in the first version, punctuates the revision. He makes the gesture repeatedly, and he dies upon it after that long run that laminates Nixon, football, Christ, and the last image of a martyrdom that became the antireligion of Jews: "He'd become like some kind of terrifying symbol or something, . . . It was only when he'd finished his run and turned back to trot toward the cops with his arms stretched out in a V above his head that one of them shot him."

In the revision, however, Meyer is given pages upon pages of detailed development as artist, a development so detailed that Gus is almost forgotten in the middle, only to be reinstituted with a shock value that forces one to read all the layers into a single, singularly American, concoction of history. If Spain (that very particular place of the thirties' conscience) recedes into other places in Coover's revised version of Meyer's history (a recession or expansion for which Leo's name becomes metonymy), Meyer invites Nixon into the diaspora of the disenfranchised: "Both of us were far from home, fulfilling myths about ourselves, his rags-to-riches drama of the industrious American boy, mine the curse of the wandering Jew." Between the two versions, the rootless Puritan had made the Quixotic attempt of fantasy (the Jewish Ethel Rosenberg fantasized in an eroticism that could not separate itself from politics) that leads the Nixon of *The Public Burning* to Sing Sing like some knight of feudal adventures. The dream is, of course, like those before Quijote, a dream of pattern-breaking, of antigeneric freedom at last, a dream of personal history. But they have memorized too much, Gus, Nixon, Meyer. They are actors, activists, artists who know all the moves, and only that. Coover's finest revision of the meaning of the first novella when he returned to it after writing *The Public Burning* was a single line. Before Meyer had known he had something in common with Gus; but he had not seen its significance for Gus's end or for his own presence as a Coover persona: "I think of myself as a lyrical socialist, which makes about as much sense, given the world we live in, as being an anal-retentive anarchist" (37). Gus died by this enigma, and Coover's career was advanced but also terribly retarded by *The*

Public Burning. In an interview from a more innocent time in his career, Coover explained that "artists . . . make us think about doing all the things we shouldn't do, all the impossible, apocalyptic things . . . weaken and tear down structures so that they can be rebuilt . . . Realizing this gave me an excuse to be the anarchist I've always wanted to be" (*First Person*, 157). Like Meyer, he was reeducated between the versions of "Gloomy Gus" to understand what he had had in hand, what he had produced. So he rewrote it with a little narrative and metaphoric coda: "which makes about as much sense, given the world we live in, as being an anal-retentive anarchist with a bomb in his hand."

Reading through the reviews of *The Public Burning* is an object lesson in the ephemerality of the present: Written during 1977, they (pro and contra) are weighted with historical dust. Aside from Geoffrey Wolff's insightful essay,[9] they illuminate what Coover said in an interview on his reading: "I assumed that the stuff that is in a sense furthest in the past — that is the most dated, irrelevant, and useless to us — is what was published last year, and that fictions become more valuable, more relevant to us as they recede in time."[10] In that same interview, Coover said that "Melville has had a very direct effect on me. By chance, I did not read *Moby Dick* until I was reworking *Brunists.* It helped me finish that book. It was a lesson on perseverance: I thought that if a writer could go that far in exploring an idea, then I could go the distance with my book" (146). That is, of course, the key to the disruption of expectation in *The Public Burning*, the nervousness it exacts from readers, exacted from its reviewers, one of whom saw the source if not the point of excess: "The Cetology chapter of *Moby Dick* provides perhaps the closest analogue to Coover's methodology."[11]

Let us begin backward, supposing that we read *The Public Burning* as children of the twenty-first century, as we here, now, read *Moby Dick*, whalers long gone and never known by most of us even in history, dreams. Or an unknown Gorky, who plays such a large, silent role in "Gloomy Gus," yet never is a character. Suppose we

9. "An American Epic," *New Times*, 19 August 1977, 49–57.
10. *First Person*, 146.
11. Robert Tower, "Nixon's Seventh Crisis," in *New York Review of Books* 29 (September 1977): 8.

could conceive a novel not about Nixon, but about ambition and doubt, about the author's loss of character in authorizing these strange people to reenter fiction, the novel, the renewableness of that form from the limited planes of history. And suppose the characters' reexistence on this new plane was precisely the point, the author's "scholarship," "research" a lesson in sacrifice, a trial to find out what they had tried to find out, what the plot attempted to identify: Who they might have been if they had not been who they were. Let us suppose the novel was written by a historical character whose presence is forgotten before the writing. Is this not the context, the area of observation that any veristic, historical fiction demands? Nixon was calculated to be unknown even at this little distance from the novel's origins. *The Public Burning* is a historical novel, then, in an almost random sense: Neither the author/narrator nor the historical narrator, not to speak of the main event, which is removed to pure metaphor — none of these have other than vehicular presence in the novel. Let us, then, search out their tenor.

As literally as one or two of Coover's short stories, much more so than the political shows in *A Political Fable*, the setting of *The Public Burning* is a circus. Times Square has been rigged out as a giant "set" with adjunct attractions (the movies, the bands, the whale from Disney's *Pinocchio*, the grand entrance parade of the whole cast involved in the Rosenbergs' trial, climaxing with the Republican elephant). Hoopla and bunting, and the principals' not-quite-death-defying act in the fiery light show at the center. As Coover said in retrospect: "All that has happened that day happens there, in a way; everything is condensed into one big circus event. Originally, it was the circus aspect that interested me most." [12] After the book was published, he was more specific about its rising tempo and its principal narrator: "My interest in Nixon — or my story about him — grew out of my concept of the book as a sequence of circus acts. That immediately brought to mind the notion of clown acts, . . . You have a thrilling high-wire number, and then the clown comes on . . . takes a pratfall, drops his pants and exits. And then you can throw another high-wire act at them. So naturally I looked for the clownish aspects of my narrator, and you can't have an unsympathetic

---

12. *First Person*, 155. Thomas LeClair's essay develops this notion.

clown . . . But in truth, with Nixon it didn't feel unnatural."[13]

One reason it might not have done lies as much in Richard Nixon's history as in his character: As a young man he had served (it is a memory that recurs to him throughout the novel) as a "carny barker" for a "wheel of chance" (175) (and that particular device is metaphoric of his entire search for pattern). But the word *circus* and the institution it suggests are both late epicycles around that more mysterious event called *carnival.* The circus is spectacular, prearranged, an entertainment, above all, commercial, safe. The ringmaster is in charge; the lions are leashed, not at bay in their lair.[14] But carnival, in all of its manifestations, is an event: contingent, tribal, renewing. It is chaos, alive and potentially deadly; Saturnalian scapegoats came after the murder of real kings. What Nixon gradually comes to understand is just that — this is no mere circus but carnival American-style, a sexual orgy and a blood bath in which he aspired to be king. He plays many roles but this is a very dangerous game. He has given himself to a ritual that only Uncle Sam Slick understands: the American "civil religion."

> The great white way. Coming here's like attending church. The American church, I mean.
> — Robert Coover

> I have always been interested in the American civil religion. I wondered where the roots of it were, of this heresy of Western Christianity, why it developed, and why we don't recognize it or talk about it. Durkheim's constructs gave me valuable insights and led me to other reading about primitive societies in which festivals were set up in order to return us to dream time.
> — Robert Coover

13. "An American Epic," 54.
14. Coover explores the limits and dangers of this conception in another "romance," "The Romance of the Thin Man and the Fat Lady," in *P&D,* 138–49.

"Dream time": Coover's Nixon dreams literally and metaphorically. An area to return to.[15] But Coover need not have been so mystified about our civil religion (the term is Rousseauesque). Robert Bellah, at least, had talked about it while *The Public Burning* was in progress, and had done so in such a way as to clarify, even make seem inevitable, the ritual Sam sets at the climax of *The Public Burning*, and to lead us past it into the larger and more interesting question of carnival and the novel.

Let us begin by quoting a little from observations, from texts cited by this liberal theologian writing within the context of American history, which was the spawning ground of *The Public Burning*. John F. Kennedy first, from his inaugural address: "a celebration of freedom — symbolizing an end as well as a beginning — signifying renewal as well as change"; Bellah's endorsement drew enough fire to elicit his response: "I defend myself against the accusation of supporting an idolatrous worship of the American nation." [16] I cite an intelligent and humane essay from and upon American history, and, whether Coover knew it or not, an essay that anticipates the historical understructure of *The Public Burning* when Bellah suggests that "the words and acts of the founding fathers, especially the first few presidents, shaped the form and tone of the civil religion as it has been maintained ever since" (175). Yes, but, Bellah continues to argue, the God-oriented (but never specifically Christian) religion of American mythology took up a new ritual at the Civil War (a similar thing happened within the politics of *The Universal Baseball Association, Inc.*): "A new theme of death, sacrifice, and rebirth enters the civil religion" (177). Then Bellah lets the old European shibboleths emerge, those that are put under caustic examination in the *Crucible* scenes of *The Public Burning* where Arthur Miller resigns himself to Puritanism ("Puritanism!" says Uncle Sam, "whoo, worse 'n acne! It's great for stirrin' up the jism when you're nation-breedin, but it ain't no way to live a life" [*PB*, 531]). "The earliest symbolism of the civil religion had been Hebraic without in any specific sense being Jewish" (178). Perhaps; but there is in Nixon's head, in Coover's novel, the

---

15. *Charlie in the House of Rue* (Lincoln, Mass., 1980) is a novella narrating the bad dream of another "clown," Charlie Chaplin. See chapter V below.

16. Robert N. Bellah, *Beyond Belief: Essays on Religion in a Post-Traditional World* (New York, 1970), 168. All subsequent citations are to this edition.

sensuous Jew ("Hell, I got a touch of kike in me myself, son . . . just enough for a little color and wile," Sam says [PB, 88]), the Puritan Pat.

As he completes his exploration, Bellah could be writing an epigraph for The Public Burning, a commentary upon Coover's various statements about the "church" of Times Square and its great festival: "Behind the civil religion at every point lie biblical archetypes: Exodus, Chosen People, Promised Land, New Jerusalem, and Sacrificial Death and Rebirth. But it is also genuinely American and genuinely new" (186).

And Bellah might have been writing a capsule review when he spoke of the Truman and Dulles era's sense of world pattern as "the great Manichean confrontation of East and West, the confrontation of democracy and 'the false philosophy of Communism'" (184).

Coover's circus is directed, his carnival invested with this American, human attempt to recall the heresy of dichotomies into light and dark, but the monological novel has given way to the dialogic. Let us remember that a word frequently appearing in The Public Burning was revised out of "Gloomy Gus": In the first version we hear that the skeptical Harry is a "poet and a Trotskyite, and he loves paradox" (46). There is a good deal of that in the relationship between Sam and the Phantom in the novel. But in the revised version of "Gloomy Gus," "paradox" is replaced by "enigma," in homage, I think, to Coover's awakened awareness of what his great novel had been about.

It is not that Robert Coover does not exist in The Public Burning; he exists in dozens of allusions to his former novels, to his own novelistic obsessions: Harry Gold's parlor baseball game [124], the numerologies that settle upon multiples of seven ("fourteen," the key misleading number of The Origin of the Brunists, is here also a miscue, as the Rosenbergs do not die — as that other anticipated apocalypse did not come — on that date). The old West of the play The Kid is here, complete with the "peace train" and the "deputy" who so much disturbs its dramatic structure (239–40). But these avatars of Coover exist as Nixon and the rest exist, as allusions to a history that has no interpreter. The novel incorporates at times a dialogue about history (Ethel's operetta with Ike), but more usually it supplies an immense cacophany of views, overlapping of voices that wedge Coover out as a bit singer in his own chorale. Nixon has no more privilege than the author, though he is so desperately trying to listen into history's conversation. The self-inclusion/exclusion of Coover the author, the refusal to privilege the "central" voice of Nixon even while the plot does center on his experience — these are the important markings by which we can begin to identify *The Public Burning*.

I have been describing a fiction that is not an authorial monologue, not even a dialogue between author and character(s), not even between characters structurally freed from authorship by way of dramatic form, a voice set into the scenario of debate under the deterministic rubric of tragedy or comedy (although this form is inset within the larger structure of *The Public Burning*). It is, rather, a pure embodiment of what Mikhail Bakhtin envisioned when he discerned the evolution of fiction toward the "dialogic" novel. The importance and originality of both the critic and the novelist, their seizure upon the essence of originality always (and, in our time, only) resident in the novel, is underlined by the lack of any linkage between them. There is no hint in interviews or reviews that Coover is aware of Bakhtin. At this date, it is improbable that he is not, in at least a casual way; but, when *The Public Burning* was begun, none of Bakhtin's books was available in the West. By the time we had absorbed the Rabelais and received translations of the studies in the novel, *The Public Burning* was a fully developed work.[17]

But Bakhtin and Coover are emblematic of the one shared struggle that unites critic and creator when so many of their needs separate them. In his small way (and we have to remember that even a Bakhtin offers nothing but echoes he has heard from pages of the past), the critic struggles against norms as the novelist struggles against norms. Bakhtin tried to circumvent this struggle by starting his history of the emergence of the novel at an idealized, arbitrary beginning of the genre: Heliodorus's romance. Coover, too, must

17. For bibliographical detail I refer to Michael Holquist's edition of *The Dialogic Imagination: Four Essays* (Austin, 1981), xxxiii–xxxiv; the Russian version of the Dostoevsky study of 1929 was a lost book until 1963; the Rabelais study did not surface until 1965, and was translated as *Rabelais and His World* in 1968; *Problems of Dostoevsky's Poetics* was translated and published in 1973. Julia Kristeva did some minor essays in French as early as 1967. Coover does not read Russian and could have learned little of interest from Kristeva had he happened upon her comments.

imagine an ancient Greek beginning: Aesop. To create within a genre, one must imagine it exists.

Aristotle first, then his Renaissance commentators, expansionists did this job of work for the drama, for the epic, and gave Shakespeare and Milton something to deconstruct. But modern fiction began, attained independent status with Boccaccio, and he contributed to the problem of future fictional forms by refusing to offer the Renaissance critics anything to incorporate into their generic dicta. While thousands of pages were dedicated to imitations of Boccaccio, none challenged his limitations, because he did not involve his work in an anachronistic Aristotelianism, which he could not have imagined. But he did address it in terms that erased fiction from the hierarchy of genres until the nineteenth century: "In these stories will be found adventures of love both happy and grievous, and other accidents of fortune as well in times present as in days of old . . . stories or fables or parables or histories or whatever you choose to style them."[18]

There simply was, in this, nothing to grapple with for the categorical minds who created mass practical criticism in the Renaissance. So they continued to multiply genres within the challenges of the old confines: The debate over Ariosto (epic or romance), the debate (inaugurated by Guarini himself, author of a genre with a single member) about tragicomedy and *its* relationship to romance.

But, like Coover's, Bakhtin's next heritage is from the Renaissance, Rabelais as Bakhtin's carnivalesque litterateur, Cervantes as Coover's epistemological storyteller. They follow, trace, expand a history of a new thing, a history of the multiple relations between life and story which never quite have become formulated in genres: "The novel," Bakhtin realizes at last, at this distance from its beginnings, "appears to be a creature from an alien species. It gets on poorly with the other genres. It fights for its own hegemony in literature; wherever it triumphs, the other older genres go into decline" (*Dialogic*, 4; Coover will reexamine the alien's entry in *ANM*.).

It is Dostoevsky's late arrival, the need of a modern to wrestle with generic history, that gives Bakhtin an even greater sympathy

---

18. Boccaccio, *Decameron*, trans. John Payne, rev. Charles S. Singleton (Berkeley, 1982), 1:5 (a passage that concludes "o historie che dire le vogliamo" in the *Decameron*, ed. Vittore Branca [Florence, 1950], 1:6).

for the novelist than he displays for Rabelais. Rabelais was given the rich stuff of folk forms to mold into a Menippean mélange of motifs; Dostoevsky had to circumvent the structural limits that had grown up around the novel as a *monologic* structure. By this term, Bakhtin indicates expressions of ideas that are not expressions of an entire world view vying with other world views. Ideas are not, in this sense epistemological, which is a violation of a central function: "When the novel becomes the dominant genre, epistemology becomes the dominant discipline" (*Dialogic*, 15). The monologic author uses the hero or others as spokesmen, but their ideas "gravitate toward the symmetrically monologic worldview of the author himself . . . a thought is either affirmed or repudiated; otherwise it simply ceases to be a fully valid thought" (*Dostoevsky*, 79–80). This is at the opposite extreme of presentational form from Coover's self-removal from the voices of *The Public Burning*.

If this struggle with the temptations of form was successful in freeing Dostoevsky from a monologic viewpoint, it is not *because* he writes formless novels, but *how* he treats form. Tolstoy also inhabited Bakhtin's immediately precedent world of the novel, but his sprawling structures were examples of the old novel, an energetic if irrelevant rival.[19] To understand that "how" we must ask more about the not immediately obvious path that leads Bakhtin from Rabelais to Dostoevsky. Or, put in a way that encompasses Rabelais, Dostoevsky, and Coover, we must return to carnival. And carnival always, of course, conducts us quickly again to dream. As a young man, Dostoevsky reported his experience of the great city of St. Petersburg as "a fantastic magical daydream":

Suddenly I saw strange faces . . . Someone *grimaced* in front of me, hiding behind that *fantastic crowd*, and *jerked at some strings and springs*, and these *puppets* moved, and he guffawed, how he guffawed! . . . if one could gather together that whole crowd which I dreamed of then, it would make a wonderful masquerade.[20]

19. For Bakhtin's contrast, see esp. *Dostoevsky*, 69–75. Tolstoy's is a Joycean world, if we are using large multiform novels as touchstones: "That external world in which the characters of the story live and die is the *author's world*, an objective world vis-à-vis the consciousness of the characters. Everything in it is seen and portrayed in the author's all-encompassing and omniscient field of vision" (71).

20. Ibid., 160–61, citing "Petersburg Dreams," 1861.

Dostoevsky was good at dreams, nightmares, as is Coover. But the carnival image here is a little isolated, distanced from the narratives. There are disguises, charades, but not properly that "masquerade" associated with the carnivalesque. Dostoevsky's world was not populated by Coover's "clowns," but Rabelais' was. The entire thrust of Bakhtin's exploration in *Rabelais and His World* is toward the definition of the "carnivalesque"; it is a central notion that reemerges in *Problems of Dostoevsky's Poetics*, and that leads far behind Rabelais to the Menippean form, which is, in Bakhtin's ultimate view, not simply the origin, but in paradoxical ways both the ur-form and the ideal form, of the "dialogic" novel.

Many forms of the "carnivalistic" originally were, of course, associated with carnival. Bakhtin reminds us that in the great medieval cities — Rome, Venice, Paris, Nuremberg, Cologne — the citizens "lived a full carnival life on the average of three months out of the year":

> It could be said . . . that a person of the Middle Ages lived, as it were, *two lives*: one was the *official* life, monolithically serious and gloomy, subjugated to a strict hierarchical order, full of terror, dogmatism, reverence, and piety; the other was the *life of the carnival square*, free and unrestricted, full of ambivalent laughter, blasphemy, the profanation of everything sacred, full of debasing and obscenities . . . Both these lives were legitimate, but separated by strict temporal boundaries. (*Dostoevsky*, 129–30)

With the Renaissance there came a weaker but recognizable line of court and class entertainments, "the *masquerade line* of development," in which echoes of license "were completely cut off from their folk base and left the public square" to enter the chamber (*Dostoevsky*, 130–31); it is, one might say, the nineteenth-century line of development, the line of Dostoevsky and Poe.

Even here, though, Bakhtin can find the relevant form that passed from carnival to "carnivalization." Dostoevsky abandoned the evolutionary structure for "*coexistence* and *interaction*. He saw and conceived his world primarily in terms of space, not time . . . to get one's bearings on the world meant to conceive all its contents as simultaneous, and *to guess at their interrelationships in the cross-section of a single moment*" (*Doestoevsky*, 28). This act of juxtaposing high and low, turning worlds into a myriad atomic world views whirling in a gathered space to create a world view, one from many, a view of the world never enunciated by the author: This is, of course, the spatial metaphor for the "dialogic" novel.

But it was for Coover to seize upon this "spatial form" and return it, in testing America's "civil religion," to the critical moment of celebration in the old place whence it had come, "the carnival square," the biggest of them all, Times Square. If *The Public Burning* is a carefully constructed, almost hour-by-hour temporal account of those three days leading up to the executions (the "High Noon" inset chapter is metonymy for the whole temporal sense of inexorability which is one of the novel's most powerful latent features, a subconscious rush that battles the endless ticking off of details), this scheme is funneling everything toward the great carnival in Times Square. The carnival must find its moment of propitiation to strange and savage gods, when Ethel Rosenberg's body — complete with the synonym[21] that moves this action for its moment from the two-dimensional page out into a fuller space — is

whipped like a sail in a high wind, flapping out at the people like one of those trick images in a 3-D movie . . . Her body, sizzling and popping like firecrackers, . . . burns — as though held aloft by her own incandescent will and haloed about by all the gleaming great of the nation. (*PB*, 517)

This is a long, long narratological way both backward and forward in the history of the novel from the nineteenth century, even that of the Dostoevsky for whom Bakhtin becomes cicerone. If one can set the truly "dialogic" novel against Joyce's controlled remythologizing, and in that sense see Coover in a different tradition, in this squeezing of dense space into brief narrative time, this chorus in a space dense with "realities," his own and Joyce's modernist form seem similar in other important ways.[22] And to conceive just how far in the past Coover's narrative is rooted, we might begin by

21. The physicality and grotesqueness are developed at length in the holocaust section, where the "mad moviegoer" forgets to remove his 3-D glasses upon leaving the theater (281–88). There is a thorough exploration relating this segment to the novel in Louis Gallo, "Nixon and the 'House of Wax,'" *Critique* 23, no. 3 (1982): 43–51.
22. It may be appropriate to notice that the myth-making last chapter of *UBA* echoes the student joking in jargon that goes on as underside to the parallel group discussion of life, death, birth, and rebirth among the young men gathered in the "Oxen of the Sun" section of *Ulysses*.

seeing Coover's Times Square as the novelist's fantastic reconstruction of the "official" (as opposed to merely carnival) space that Bakhtin describes as the chronotope for one sort of time-space interaction that went back before medieval separations began: "The square in earlier (ancient) times itself constituted a state (and more — it constituted the entire state apparatus, with all its official organs), it was the highest court, the whole of science, the whole of art, the entire people participated in it" (*Dialogic*, 132). Well, Coover's Uncle Sam has gathered them here, from the Supreme Court to the Marx Brothers, for the final judgment and show. That his carnival turns into a circus is the primary responsibility of its self-selected protagonist, who, after all, is not that scapegoat angel of light Ethel, but the clown Richard Nixon. And it is with Nixon that one must test Coover's unconscious testing of both the rightness and the limits of Bakhtin's insistence upon the suprageneric, cannibalistic nature of the novel form. And, in particular, the relationship fantasy bears to history, a subject that by a wide circle will bring us eventually back to the implications inherent in the notion that "when the novel becomes the dominant genre, epistemology becomes the dominant discipline."

Let us indulge briefly in recapitulating Bakhtin's imaginative (and necessarily imaginary) recapitulation of history. In the beginning there were two rival literatures, reflections of those two cultures he rediscovered later in the public square (always, one notes, identified as "ancient") and the carnival square (always implicitly a later cultural phenomenon, that which came after the founders, the fathers of the cultures we still identify with western fiction, history, politics, religion). But in their literary counterparts, they coexisted from the beginning (wherever that may have been in the battle between light and dark, laughter and grimness, Gloomy Gus and the clown): These literary traditions were the heroic epic and what Bakhtin often labels with modern shorthand "menippean," but the generic word is broader more precisely descriptive: *spoudogeloios*, the serio-comic (*Dostoevsky*, 106–22; *Dialogic*, 3–40; etc.). The latter was a continuation of folk laughter into parodic written genres: dreams, confessions, letters, dialogues with the dead and the living, the panoply of imaginable and imagined discourses which the ancient world had with the claims of history, which it shored against the rigid threats of historic form as soon (what do we know?) as such forms arose.

As novelistic tendencies emerged into separably discernible, although obviously overlapping, forms, there emerged the Greek romance. It is familiar to most of us most clearly in its late Menandrian/Plautine form of New Comedy: the young lovers blocked and regrouping to overcome difficulties and reform (or, better, reformulate) societies. But there are certain features that are not so apparent in the dramatic heritage, and the most important of these is that the metaphor of "meeting" by which narrative draws the lovers to destiny, even tragic destiny, and all that occurs on the labyrinthine paths by which that meeting comes to be, is acted out on a spatial plane without detail, because it develops only through a "logic" of "*random contingency* . . . which is to say, chance *simultaneity* [meetings] and *chance rupture* [nonmeetings], that is, a logic of random *disjunctions* in time as well" (*Dialogic*, 92).

It is too early to distract ourselves more than momentarily with applications of taxonomy to Coover's practice in the compendium of *The Public Burning*. But it may not be a distraction so much as a suggestion as to where things may lead to set Nixon's growing love fantasy about Ethel Rosenberg into even such a rough reduction of Bakhtin's account of the primitive novel. This is to be reminded that one late, major strand of *The Public Burning* is a love story that threatens to rob Uncle Sam of his predestined lover. As he expands rough experiential similarities (which would have been shared by almost any bourgeoise victim of the American depression of the thirties in remembering a childhood), Nixon begins to understand Ethel, to yearn to tell her (he even sees how he might have been Julius with a little bad luck [139]) of the meaning of it all. Imposing pattern, he determines upon the meeting at Sing Sing. He chanced in at the wrong time, of course, as he does so often: disjunction, and the new questioning of the assumed patterns. But this section of *The Public Burning*, with Nixon's decision to go upstate from New York City on the holiday train; with the transformation, once he arrives; the revision of the orgiastic train fantasy into a meticulous description of verifiable landscape hedging into the *Liebestod* meeting outside the death chamber; all of this can lead us back by way of what we know about Nixon to see that Coover has stepped across the border of the

Greek romances of chance into Bakhtin's second version of the novel in the ancient world, the "travel novel," wherein we have at the center "the *author's real homeland.*" It is a generic or subgeneric revision in which all (the mistake about Ethel, about the Phantom?) else, "alien countries and cultures are seen and understood . . . In this sense of a native country in itself . . . an internal organizing center for seeing and depicting that is located 'at home' — [and] radically changes the entire picture of a foreign world" (*Dialogic*, 103–4). Now, while the "travel novel" is a version of the Greek romance in its more contingent love-quest form, it is in this respect crucially altered. If in the earlier form foreign territories are without features other than a distance of separation, the travel novel *must* possess them to become a testing: If the landscape is the *patria*, the character who traverses it must be a patriot. At Sing Sing, Nixon (inevitably disguised as a clown) almost faltered into a private dream. But even then it was not to save Ethel alone, or even primarily, but to surprise Sam and turn around history. He soon repents and returns to Times Square for the great moment he has not yet understood except as a test he is willing to face. This returns our survey to Bakhtin at an important juncture in the description of this new old Greek novel:

This private and isolated man of the Greek romance quite often behaves, on the surface, like a public man, . . . He delivers long speeches that are rhetorically structured and in which he seeks to enlighten us with the private and intimate details of his love life, his exploits and adventures — but all this not in the form of an intimate confession — rather in the form of a *public accounting.* (*Dialogic*, 108–9)

Such an accounting marked the historical Nixon's encounters with America from the first, always "making it perfectly clear": the "Checkers" speech; *Six Crises*; "I'm not a crook"; to the final resignation speech. And he goes a little beyond in Coover's Times Square.

I think we can learn much about Coover's structural encyclopedism from watching, at appropriate times, the details with which his structure cannibalizes or preempts Bakhtin's encyclopedia of observations about significant elements that gather around this and all other nuclear novelistic subgenres. However, let us get on to completing the anatomy of Bakhtin's essays in comparative fictions.

The travel novel, for an important difference, he insists, depends upon the journey, "the *itinerary*," as an organizing principal of the "adventure" structure, which this form shares with the contingent, chance junctures and disjunctures of the romance form. And this, in turn, along with the public testing of the protagonist, places him in time, a terrible time, a time of puzzlement as he tries to get past those aspects of this test which seem to accuse his attempts to adjust public and private, grand adventurer and local traveler — seem to accuse him in these attempts as a disguise artist, as a practitioner of "*presumed betrayal* (with subsequent confirmation of unswerving fidelity)," until in the end such structures achieve "the basic compositional (that is, organizing) motif of *a test of the heroes' integrity, their selfhood*. In all these instances the narrative plays directly with *traits of human identity*" (*Dialogic*, 104–6). Now this is not new since wily Ulysses, and Leopold Bloom. But what about such a fellow traveler who would also "be occupied primarily with the task of becoming conscious, the sort of hero whose life would be concentrated on the pure function of gaining consciousness of himself and the world" (*Dostoevsky*, 50). They are apparently distinct beings, these, the public apologist, the "patriot," if one may so call him, and the Dostoevskian self-examiner, and they play different roles in different divisions in Bakhtin's historical, formal economies of the novel.

This seeming bifurcation of character within his landscape, however, leads us back to Coover and his Nixon, who is public orator and self-inquisitor at once (the complicated problem for the author which forced him to take pause and avoidance by redoing the model as the simplified "Gloomy Gus").

Bakhtin never faced the problem of this convergence, but moved on to write about Dostoevsky, in whose "artistic thinking, the genuine life of the personality takes place at the point of non-coincidence between a man and himself" (*Dostoevsky*, 59). But Coover imagined himself into a searching, self-conscious being who would yet conclude (not only once in the course of *The Public Burning*) that he *was* really, and *knew what was* really (the novel invites epistemology, to recall), in a phenomenological sense. He felt only what came in from out there. And then in that last stand upon the fiery circus stage of Times Square when, having come from his encounter with inner fantasies about, and outer disaster with, Ethel in Sing Sing (his am-

bivalent move toward privacy), he stood bared on the carnival platform of Times Square and decided that the inner consciousness he
had been seeking was, had always been (as we, he more than half-
knew throughout) public. He was Uncle Sam's boy. But Bakhtin offers us the clue to possible complications even he did not foresee, I
think, when he adapts as central to the next stage of the Greek
adventure novel, that best known through Apuleius and Petronius, a
highly charged word that is a recurrent note when Coover discusses
his own work: "metamorphosis."

   In the early interview explaining the geneses of his fictions,
Coover remarked upon the effect of rereading Ovid:

The Ovidian stories all concern transformation; now that is not a startlingly
new subject — after all, fairy tales, animal fables, and the like, deal with
it — but I suddenly realized that the basic constant struggle for all of us is
against metamorphosis, against giving in to the inevitability of the process.
(*First Person*, 152)

   These are just the sorts of folk and poetic resources which Bakhtin
insists channel into the "adventure novel of everyday life." In this
type it is "precisely the course of the hero's . . . life in its critical
moments that makes up the plot of the novel" (*Dialogic*, 111), a type
preserved and epitomized in Apuleius's *Metamorphoses*, which we
have happily come to know by its rich subtitle, *The Golden Ass*. But
the life is "sheathed in the context of a 'metamorphosis,'" that context
which Coover finds inevitable and resisted. Resisted, because it is a
dangerous matter, a matter of altering the human identity. Now this
is reduced to a rather simple matter in the Ovidian tales. If young
Hyacinthus at a critical encounter with the gods becomes metamorphosed into a flower, he does not go about worrying his condition as
does Apuleius' man-ass Lucius; Ovidian "characters" absorb their
crucial change into their new natural state as far from threatening;
as, rather, the reassuring process of repetitious resurrection: They
triumph in that mythic immortality of nature.

   In the Apuleian type of adventure novel, the protagonist also
undergoes "crisis and rebirth." But it is of a psychological sort:

Metamorphosis serves as the basis for a method of portraying the whole of
an individual's life in its more important moments of *crisis*: for showing *how
an individual becomes other than what he was* . . . This is not, therefore, a

biographical life, in its entirety. In the crisis-type of portrayal we see only one or two moments that decide the fate of a man's life and determine its entire disposition. (*Dialogic,* 115)

Well, perhaps with self-aggrandizement, Richard Nixon, of course, discerned the shape of his life to have involved — it is the title of his prepresidential autobiography — *Six Crises.* Coover consistently employs the psychology and frequently the words of this extraordinary book; I bring to attention two brief instances that reveal Nixon's awareness of the situation Coover's arrangement has placed him in as being that of a seventh prepresidential crisis: "Life for everyone is a series of crises, I cautioned myself, it's not just you" (*PB,* 87). Knowing so much, it is the psychology of "crisis" itself which he tries to master: "Is it possible to be rational at all in crisis situations? Do crises seem to have many elements in common? Does the participant seem to learn from one crisis to another?" (*PB,* 470).[23] This is not a casual query, received either from the constantly self-exonerating, self-doubting former president of the United States, or from the Nixon of *The Public Burning.* If the Greek romance of the first type bore "chance" as its distinguishing plot mark, in the more sophisticated Apuleian novel, chance, of course, continues to enter, "but the power of chance and the initiative that lies with it is limited." Things happen to Lucius as ass by accident, but the accidents occur because character has brought him to the wrong places for the wrong reasons, so that *"he himself is guilty . . .* The *primary initiative . . .* belongs to *the hero himself* and to his own personality" (*Dialogic,* 116). If the historical incumbent struggling against impeachment shocked a nation by proclaiming before it, "I'm not a crook," Coover's Nixon delivers the analogue when he shows Times Square the asinine message "I AM A SCAMP."

Character *was* destiny for Richard Nixon in the Watergate crisis. But in *The Public Burning,* Coover leads him a long, harried way to safety. This journey, like that of Lucius, is the essence of plot structure in *The Public Burning,* and its paradox is analogous to that, mentioned a short time back, of combining the public orator and self-inquisitor in one character. It will function in *The Public Burning*

23. The latter a direct citation from p. xiii of the introduction to *Six Crises* (Garden City, N.Y., 1962). I am not aware of any commentator pointing out that chapter 11 of *PB* is an adaptation in parody of the "Caracas" adventure in *Six Crises.*

to knot the psychological journey to the myth that envelops it, to Coover's immensely thick space in which the American Civil Religion engulfs Nixon. But one had best begin explanations by recalling the final stage of metamorphosis in Bakhtin's description of the form of the Apuleian novel.

Like the initial link, the concluding link of the "entire adventure series . . . is not determined by chance." When the protagonist has been prepared, the presiding deity, priest, power (often through dreams and visions, those other worlds to which Coover's Nixon is so frequently subjected) becomes his patron, "directing him to his purification, demanding from him highly detailed purifying rituals and *askesis*" (117). Uncle Sam's directions to Nixon are strange, indeed, coming in the form mostly of conundrums, riddles, and doubts; his ascetic demands stranger still. But their relationship is clearly that of Apuleius's Lucius and the goddess Isis. The peccant puppet Pinocchio (who also plays a role in the Times Square ritual) had to become an ass as literally as does Lucius, and undergo a transformation by water, before he could become a boy or, leading old father Geppetto out of the whale's belly, become the son-become-father. It is not, of course, a casual metaphor, and inevitably entered the language; Nixon will have to make an ass of himself as literally as the others. This brings us back to the carnivalistic world turned upside down.

Having surveyed the literary origins of the novel, Bakhtin returns to the "carnival square" to discover that three archetypical characters of its production had escaped into the novel: the rogue, the clown, and the fool.[24] These figures bring the theatricality, the "mask of the public spectacle" into the space of the novel, into its public.

I think Bakhtin did not wholly grasp his own oxymoron of the public orator/private inquisitor at this point, associating these novelistic figures without seeing how far the ideal dialogic novelist could take them. Let us probe into the various ways they seem to mediate between public and private spheres, between the historical

---

24. In the interview with McCaffrey, Coover explained one avenue by which he came to choose Nixon as protagonist: "It was another quality . . . that first called him forth in my mind . . . his peculiar talent for making a fool of himself . . . [And] I was developing this series of circus acts — all of these verbal acrobatics . . . and I needed a clown to break in from time to time and do a few pratfalls. He was perfect for this" ("Coover," 59).

and fantastic. This trio can be understood only "metaphorically. Sometimes their significance can be reversed — but one cannot take them literally, because they are not what they seem" (*Dialogic*, 159). They are not, because they are not masqueraders, but exist only as masks. They are, for themselves and the others, the source of laughter, because "they re-establish the public nature of the human figure: the entire being of characters such as these is . . . utterly on the surface; everything is brought out onto the square" (*Dialogic*, 160). They are "in life, but not of it, life's perpetual spy and reflector," who can make private life public ("for example, the sexual sphere") (*Dialogic*, 161). Bakhtin views this aspect of character (or characterless) entry into the novel as a great breakthrough for the novelist on his way toward the "dialogic" form. Choosing to efface his presence from the novel and from the society it reflects or embodies, he too can spy out its secrets from the sidelines by donning such a metaphoric mask.

But one small loophole, a little flawed fact prior to theory, lets Coover's Nixon slip through, and makes havoc of the notion of authorial "spying" upon his own world. "The rogue," admits Bakhtin, "still has some ties that bind him to real life" (159). Exactly the complicating case in *The Public Burning*. Nixon is clown and fool, but he is also the rogue who will become the principal focus of public society, who will do it by publicly sacrificing the private man because society seemed to — Uncle Sam seemed to — relegate his flatness to the sidelines. This Gloomy Gus had more persistence, flatness turned out to have more surfaces, than Bakhtin had bargained for. Coover's protagonist is much too complicated to be used as front man for any authorial organization (one will need Uncle Sam for that). If one made a sequence it would run: private rogue become public clown become private rogue-clown become public rogue-clown. An obvious if awkward plot summary, were it not for the fool who accompanies them both — rogue and clown — right to the penultimate moment of the novel only at that moment — as in *Lear* — to abandon their madness.

Bakhtin's "fool," of course, is folly as wisdom; but an asocietal wisdom that can speak truth so long as it is spoken from outside. Coover did not mean this when he spoke of Nixon's folly in the interview. But he meant this when he created a Nixon wise about private selves and public folly until he succumbed to his desire to follow the circus. Or to lead it.

The Public Burning is, of course, a *historical novel* in the sense that this vague term has developed a large corpus since Norman Mailer's *Armies of the Night* and even a considerable theoretical literature that spills over into, and has been instructed by, metahistorical theorizing. So much has been said about the historical narrative and the narratology of history in general that even the best pioneering work now sounds banal, in the same tone as do, for important examples, the return to those other once-exciting foci of narrative and the signified: appearance versus reality, and metafiction. This is true because the problems, or fields of attention, had to be raised to sophisticate the continuing discourse on narrative. But they turned out to be false problems, too, no matter how necessary and honorable the attempts to embrace them; false because the parameters turned out upon examination to be coterminous with narrative itself. Like genres, though, these theoretical problems-in-the-air of modern criticism offer the artist something to react to, transmute into new shapes the theoreticians had not anticipated. Let these remarks serve as an introduction to the "itinerary" of Richard Nixon through the crisis of The Public Burning.

Coover's book is historical, and Nixon is a historical figure whose life and career he had researched, as I have said, in strenuous, sometimes obsessive, detail over several years, as he had the wider network of detail for Nixon's time of vice-presidency under Dwight D. Eisenhower, the "time" of the novel, 1953. Coover has described in retrospect the method by which "historicity" was guaranteed:

One of the peculiarities of The Public Burning was that it was made up of thousands upon thousands of tiny fragments that had to be painstakingly stitched together, and it was not hard to lose patience with it. It was like a gigantic impossible puzzle. I was striving for a text that would seem to have been written by the whole nation through all its history, as though the sentences had been forming themselves all this time, accumulating all this experience — I wanted thousands of echoes, all the sounds of a nation. Well, the idea was good, but the procedures were sometimes unbelievably tedious.[25]

25. Ibid.

The "prologue" begins with exemplary factuality in setting out the historical "argument" of the entire work (in the sense that Milton, gave the "argument" summarizing each book of *Paradise Lost*, only to surprise us with the latent content that could emerge):

On June 24, 1950, less than five years after the end of World War II, the Korean War begins, American boys are again sent off in uniforms to die for Liberty, and a few weeks later, two New York City Jews, Julius and Ethel Rosenberg, are arrested by the FBI and charged with having conspired to steal atomic secrets and pass them to the Russians. They are tried, found guilty, and on April 5, 1951, sentenced by the Judge to die — thieves of light to be burned by light — in the electric chair, for it is written that "any man who is dominated by demonic spirits to the extent that he gives voice to apostasy is to be subject to the judgment upon sorcerers and wizards." Then, after the usual series of permissible sophistries, the various delaying moves and light-restoring counter-moves, their fate — as the U.S. Supreme Court refuses for the sixth and last time to hear the case, locks its doors, and goes off on holiday — is at last sealed, and it is determined to burn them in New York City's Times Square on the night of their fourteenth wedding anniversary, Thursday, June 18, 1953. (3)

The facts are there, the voice is that of the annalist, who traces out the events until, in the same voice (nothing surprises it, not demonic judgments, sophistries, vacations), he accepts the intersection of history and fantasy to which he is offering the argument, accepts into the annals this event somehow skewed in Coover's recounting (but this is not the annalist's job, to sort these distinctions through): "it is determined to burn them in New York City's Times Square."

From this beginning, *The Public Burning* develops into the fleshing out of this argument in thirty segments, alternately pieced together from the voice of the annalist quoting the accumulated "sounds of a nation," and articulated by Richard Nixon in search of his role. In the structuring of these alternating accounts of the development of America's Civil Religion (the Rosenberg ritual), and Richard Nixon's development into its avatar, Coover has given his implicit response to the problem of historical narratology through the accomplishment of an improbable legerdemain of inversion. He has drawn the reader into the Nixonian quest to such a degree that "everyday time," the human reality of the events are experienced acutely just in those chapters filtered through Nixon's consciousness. But these chapters are (the few grounding quotations from *Six Crises* and the speeches aside — but in these public appearances, Nixon feels, of course, least real to himself as character and so to the reader) pure fantasy. The fantastic operates on several levels, from reimagined discussions in the Senate to the extremes of the dream of Ethel and the vision of the Phantom as Cab Driver. But there is not a historical fact in the account. He has become a fantasy who is made to "feel" real.

And this against the alternate chapters of "history," the voices raised verbatim from *Time* magazine, court reports on the trial, Eisenhower's papers and speeches, and so forth, which give the impression of being total fantasy, a wild national dream heading toward nightmare because it cannot awaken to its own images. Coover has, in brief, restructured the presumed relationships between historical and fantastic fiction in this historical novel. It is now a matter of the annals revealing themselves, their "todayness," in the light of the fantasy that history always incorporates to some degree. *The Public Burning* foregrounds, as an implicit function of its radical narratological inversion, the Bakhtinian association of epistemology and the novel. Theories, indeed, any consciousness or self-consciousness of those problematic mergers between factuality and fictionality are not only irrelevant, but are not present for the reader of *The Public Burning*: For Coover's reader, history is fantasy; fantasy is history.

Let us, then, enter this segment of history with Richard Nixon at Burning Tree Golf Course on the Sunday before the three-day temporal unity of the novel begins, because the testing begins here, just at the perimeter of the itinerary. It must stand outside, not as the other flashbacks that recapitulate Nixon's life from childhood on, but as the immediate origin of the patriot's itinerary through his homeland, an itinerary that can metamorphose him at last, if he can only understand the instructions.

The private Nixon, knowing something vague about his destinies, laments from time to time that he was born with a face that masked his heroic soul incongruously ("I looked like a preacher from the day I was born. Gloomy Gus they called me" [142]; "Dirksen had a wonderfully expressive face . . . just the opposite of mine, a real clown's face" [51]; Nixon had even written his itinerant mother a love letter from her dog — the animal language of the Apuleian novel is there) (along with the rogue, the clown, hidden behind the preacher). It was just this, perhaps, that had given him such a surge in amateur theatrics in his youth: "I liked that part, the makeup. A kind of transformation comes over you, a kind of metamorphosis" (111).

So the excitement was, both for the private and public man, a sense of emotional identification when he had accompanied Eisenhower to the golf course repeatedly during recent months, only to watch the metamorphosis: "Uncle Sam . . . had dropped his mask and talked with me directly about such things as stagecraft and incarnational theory." Sam's "transmutation" is awesome to watch (and doubly tantalizing for a man who wants to be both president and his true, unmasked, self): "a loosening of all the limbs as though in sympathy with the dissolution of the features of Uncle Sam's current Incarnation" (83).

It is a long clown scene for Nixon, of course, his first real opportunity to take pratfalls before the reader. Sam questions him on the Rosenberg case; Nixon reasons; Sam scoffs. Sam's golf balls are batted in heroic arcs in the styles of half-a-dozen great baseball players (*baseball*, after all, is the great American game, not golf, as Eisenhower taught, or football, as Nixon had mistakenly surmised in the interstices between the novel and novella); Nixon divots and sweats. But he duffs the surface game because he is concentratedly coming to an understanding about what it shares with more important play: "Times Square, the circus atmosphere, the special ceremonies: form, *form*, that's what it always comes down to" (91). What matters, as Sam, not Nixon, knows, is "guilt, real guilt, [which] is like grace; some people got it, some don't" (87) (we are returned to power, to Flynn/Henry at the penultimate moment of his, their decision to turn a game into that politics which becomes a religion). Certainly the consciousness-seeking protagonist will have to come to some understanding of his necessarily sinful state, but not yet, not here in the wrestling with Sam's enigmatic demands. He sees all the other sorts of obvious portents that might connect him with the Rosenberg event,[26] but not this crucial one that tests character. He discerns all the pieces (it is a detective story, a crime Sam sets him to solve) and comes up with the correct, overriding answer to why they are

26. Numerology runs rampant in his head, the magic "fourteen" of *The Origin of the Brunists* beginning to draw his own marital chronology into juxtaposition with that of the Rosenbergs: "How many other parallels might there be?" (93).

"guilty," led to it not by trial notes, but by Sam's biblical rhetoric: They are *"Sons of Darkness! I cried"* (88).

It is the right answer, and the wrong one. Why, he might (did not now) ask, am I, a son of the Light, "guilty"? Sam tells him why, tells him about metamorphoses into public commitment, but Nixon thinks only of form (of course, he cannot anticipate Ethel's haloed body at the end). Sam begins to inject the ominous suggestion that the powers of darkness and light have an even closer relationship than mere symbiosis: "'The pact with the Phantom is no less consecratin' in its dire way then gettin' graced by Yourse Truly', said Uncle Sam, . . . 'The impure, through their presumptulous contact with the sacred, are momentaneously as lit up with this force as are the pure, and it's easy for folks to confound the two'" (89–90).

Here is a psychological economy for Nixon's generic extension into parallel plots: He is left, even after the Burning Tree encounter, with the problem of what he is expected to make of, do about, the Rosenberg case; he is left with the enigma of Uncle Sam and the incarnation—not only whether Richard Nixon will be incarnated, but whether anyone will. The first is the detective story.[27] The second is a deeper mystery, one Nixon understands more instantaneously, but only for the moment of near merger between Sam and himself (once incarnated, mortality or morality of a mythic tradition will become irrelevant to any avatar). Sam has told him that notions of sacredness are indistinguishable, then he begins again in the old energetic style: "This ain't just another ballgame, johnny, we are gonna have to fight for the reestablishment of our national *character,* . . . the last best hope of the earth—namely, *me.*" The mortal implications are overwhelming, but if Nixon receives a *frisson,* he also feels "very near the center of things." Sam confides: "'Sometimes,' he said softly, 'sometimes I almost *want* to die'" (95). Nixon shudders into a felt recognition between himself and Sam. And then they get on to the carnival, separating, only to come together again at that event. Sam gives the word to the hero about to set out after the Grail ("I felt

27. Bakhtin incorporated this form into the novel, too, before Todorov, et al.: "Various forms and varieties of the novel make use of these manifold legal and criminal categories in different ways. It suffices to mention, on the one hand, the adventure-detective novel (the investigation, clues, piecing-together of events with the help of these clues) and on the other hand the novels of Dostoevsky" (*Dialogic,* 124). Nixon, in Coover's fiction, is both Poe's detective and Dostoevsky's grand inquisitor.

swarmed about with fears and absences. Paradox. But I felt protected at the same time. I had a feeling that everything in America was coming together for the first time"): "Oh, I don't reckon we could live like this all year round . . . But we do need us an occasional peak of disorder and danger" (95).

It is just the "peak" at the Public Burning toward which Nixon's double journey must move from this initiating point, which stands outside the narrative proper.

The action that follows is a detailed account of Nixon's movements during the three preexecution days. He goes from a cabinet meeting to his office (there the better to study the trial records in order to understand Uncle Sam's desires) to his home (there to begin a narcissistic affair with Ethel Rosenberg exacerbated into reality by a dream). He participates as presiding officer in the Senate, he has a harried cab ride, he evades White House pickets, he determines to travel to Sing Sing prison to elicit love, a confession of guilt, and a new (Nixon-directed) shape to the American destiny. The dreams, visions, experiences are devastating, and they leave him on center stage at Times Square, his pants about his ankles, and all America watching the act. He snatches destiny from the absurd; but along the way, he thinks a lot of things about the character coersions he has always insisted upon making for himself as destiny and desire cohabit in a body that is now Nixon, now the potential vessel of that Public Man par excellence, the future Incarnation of America.

The initial dilemma could be characterized in generic terms: He is an epic hero wistful to be a lover in the simplest sense of romance from Bakhtin's Greek file. He meets a dying old opponent, plays the unintentional clumsy clown, and muses about his self-division: "This sudden flush of warmth, even love, toward the people I defeat. It worried me, worries me still. It could backfire someday" (47). He is right about that. It leads him to fall in love with Ethel Rosenberg. But we are assured that his danger is limited by an inner flatness of character, which has to learn emotion: "I'm always sorry when people have to die, my mother taught me this" (84). But emotion, love, is what he most desperately needs, and he first seeks it with Ethel.

It begins innocently enough as Nixon sits late at night in his office, surrounded by the piled clutter of briefs, evidence, torts, and reports that make up the government case against the Rosenbergs, sits there trying to decide what Uncle Sam wants him to learn out of it all. He is exhausted, but proud of it ("My best ideas come when I think I can't work another minute, when I literally have to drive myself to stick at the job" [113]). And in a way he is right, because this exhaustion brings him to fantasize about what he has learned of Ethel's youth as a shipping clerk and (like himself) aspiring thespian. She is sixteen; she triumphs in a prison melodrama; everyone lauds and lusts after the nubile star. So an older actor, "some bum in his midforties," takes her home, talking, being fatherly, "pushes her into a dark doorway." It is, as he says, a very rough scene, and it has two consequences. The first Nixon projects as the hapless girl's reaction and destiny: "So that's what the theatrical life is like! She becomes a Communist instead and commits espionage" (113). The second is that it will lead Nixon in his midforties to reenact the attempted rape of Ethel in the Sing Sing death house. The revery passes into dream, as Nixon nods over the (authentic) Rosenberg letters:

I sat up abruptly. I thought I'd heard it, heard her voice. A sheet of paper was stuck to my cheek. I peeled it off. "Light of my life, rose of my heart, You my beloved being kept apart from me, are the thing I hold most dear. When I see your beautiful expressive face I know we are as one." *Was this for me?* Ah no. (139)

Pagliaccio has awakened to a dream of love. And terror. Uncle Sam had given him intimations about the Phantom being an equally powerful mirror image of America. Now he has reveried, dreamt himself into the avatars of that evil, the Rosenbergs. If the gods may come in dreams, they may visit us in a more direct form:

And then suddenly I had this stunning vision of little Ethel Greenglass, about six years old, standing naked by a kitchen coalstove, pulling on a pair of white cotton panties, watched furtively by her brothers . . . I tried to shake it off . . . Then I remembered that my brothers and I always used to get dressed huddled around the kitchen stove like that in Yorba Linda . . . Mama — Mrs. Greenglass, I mean — was pregnant. (145–46)

Nixon races through the darkened corridors to the elevator, feels "something rustling in the dark space," relives his fall from a perambulator; a great maternal lap, mouth, opens to tell him the consequences of falling in love with those he has defeated, with the powers of darkness: *"The Gobble-uns'll git you ef you don't watch out!"* (146).

The fantasy escalates rather than dissipates in this dark night of

fated love. Ethel is reified into the woman who will reciprocate with
that love that Nixon has never had: Pat tormented him cruelly
throughout their courtship, his mother deserted him, his grandmother Milhous had raised him with severity and religious zeal. So
stung, he plunges on deeper into folly. After a harrowing experience
with the Phantom (to which one must recur at the appropriate narrative time), on Friday afternoon Nixon returns to his office, to the
shambles of papers he had left the night before as he fled. Now he
takes up the threads again, rereads the Rosenberg correspondence,
and suddenly projects an "insight" upon it. Ethel's letter to her husband is passionate with the loss of their enforced separation ("I see
your pale drawn face, . . . your slender boyish body and your evi-
dent suffering . . . Hold me close to you tonight, I'm so lonely"
[312]). But Nixon will turn it to his own ends, in a classic misreading:

Suddenly it occurred to me, what should have been obvious all along: she
didn't love him. She never had. She needed him, but she never loved
him . . . She had loved, yes, she was a lover, but she had no proper object
for her love . . . "Sweetheart, I draw you close into loving arms and warm
you with my warmth." She could as well have been speaking to me. (312–13)

Nixon has come a long way from the mood of the night before when,
reading these same letters, he had said: *"Was this for me? Ah no."*

Beside his obvious psychology of need, there is a mythic or
"tribal" reason for this new attitude. It is the erotic excitement
aroused by the imminence of the ritual, of the sacrificial "burning":
"If sex is dirty, it is also, at its dirtiest, cleansing; if it defiles, it also
sanctifies" (166). Nixon admits while shaving that "I hadn't completely shaken off all that happened last night. I had awakened with
an erection, for example . . . and it still hadn't gone away" (186).
But Eisenhower, too, awakens happily manic "with the handsomest
hard-on in a dog's age," and so does his assistant: "It's impossible, of
course, for Sherm Adams to know, but were a poll to be taken, he
would discover that not only he and the President, but also most of
Congress, the Supreme Court, lesser courts and commissions, the
Fourth Estate, Cecille B. De Mille and Cardinal Spellman, the Holy
Six, and the Vice President sacked out on his living-room couch . . .
have all awakened this morning from the foment of strange gamy
dreams with prodigious erections and enflamed crevices." But no one
has "used his or her aroused sexuality on a mate, it's as though,

somehow, that's not what it was all about"; rather, it is a generalized "unwonted appetite for risk and profligacy" (163–64). Well, no one will risk more than Richard Nixon. He moves from his "discovery" of Ethel's need to a reverie of how he had saved her from strike breakers in a scene from her youth, flung himself protectively on her body, undressed, admitted their mutual virginity ("'Richard,' she whispers, 'I've never . . . never . . .' 'Neither have I,' I say softly, . . . She strokes me gently, 'I draw you close into loving arms and warm you with my warmth'") — at which near-orgasmic moment the erotic dream is broken by the rival lover: "'Well, I see that the old flagpole still stands,' somebody said . . . It was Uncle Sam, who had just flown in through my open window" (318). And even yet the vice-president will not learn that he is public, not private, man.

He will persist in confusing the two spheres to the point of completely mixing incompatible motives in going to Sing Sing at the penultimate hour to persuade Ethel to confess, to make love, to change America's destiny. He disguises himself in ways that seem to attract adjacent characters: Groucho Marx (already in Times Square yacking up the festivities) and Julius Rosenberg. He arrives at the death house, he encounters Ethel at last. "Don't be afraid," he says, "It's just me, Richard Nixon" (414). Haughty, she is insulted at this raw ploy by the inquisitors, the executioners; Nixon is desperate in sincerity: "Mrs. Rosenberg — Ethel . . . This has nothing to do with the government — I've run away from the government — believe me, it's *you* I care about" (433). She shies; he becomes aggressive, beginning his reenactment of Ethel's imagined girlhood rape by exorcising caution and ambition in a single fling for freedom of will: "I didn't know what I was doing but I did know I was through being polite, I was through being Mr. Nice Guy, I was all done with trying to out-argue women, or men either, Uncle Sam included, to hell with respect and consideration" (436). Roughly he begins to overmaster her, feels "an incredible new power, a new freedom. Where did it come from? Uncle Sam? The Phantom? Both at once? From neither . . . I had escaped them both" (442). But not Ethel — or, in fact, Sam. The illusion is broken when the guards come for her, when Nixon hides in the electric chair, when the adventure is wrapped into his need for Sam. Reneging, he "ducked back out of sight, reflecting that a man who has never lost himself in a cause bigger than himself has missed one of life's mountaintop experiences: only in losing himself does he find himself." He pleads, "Ethel, forgive me." She replies, "I'll be thinking of you. Richard" (446). She does, one supposes, as she swings into the 3-D carnival of Times Square, where Nixon has to explain the motto she had written in lipstick across his ass: "I AM A SCAMP." But now he has to explain to Uncle Sam, too.

Even leaving Pat Nixon aside, this man is getting into much too complicated and contradictory a love life. But Ethel has represented only a wavering, serious, yet personal indulgence in need. And even in this relationship he had assumed he could use her confession to change the American destiny manifest in the Times Square carnival. But in whatever event, he knew that guilt, innocence, confusion were not the issues, he knew Sam to be a talker who wanted talk on this particularly holy American Friday night:

> I had to reread the letters, the biographies, search out the hidden themes, somehow reach a panoramic view of the event, and *write a speech!* That was the point: I had to go before the people tonight . . . *That* was what Uncle Sam was expecting of me! That was what language was for: to transcend the confusions, restore the spirit, recreate the society. (234)

This, then, is a summary account of the private love story, intimation of its merger into America as another kind of myth to test Nixon, to be tested by his experience or lack of it. The enveloping context is the carnivalesque event, the voices of Uncle Sam, of the American Civil Religion in which Nixon is lost, in which he hopes to find himself. Or, rather, in Coover's instance, Times Square and what Nixon must make of folly and carnival when they come to murder. One of Bakhtin's predecessors described disturbing contextualism in something like anticipation of the entire structure of *The Public Burning* as "the impulse to introduce the extraordinary into the very thick of the commonplace . . . to push images and phenomena of everyday reality to the limits of the fantastic" (*Dostoevsky*, 103). Well, here is Richard Milhous Nixon along with the rest of us, wondering what we are doing, where we are, when we are in Times Square. What we are attending, of course, is a carnival modernized into a circus, and what it is celebrating is a war between Uncle Sam and the Phantom, a Manichean carnival of lights burning against the benighted powers of darkness, to adapt Bellah's summary of new Manifest Destiny. Nixon's return to Times Square has as its chapter title "Letting Out the Dark: The Prodigal Son Returns" and as he stands upon the platform of a nation, not much pleasing Sam, he again shares (anticipates) Ethel's imminent destiny: "I could feel it all breaking down inside, like wires fusing, burning at the ends, bulbs blowing" (480). Sam is furious as Nixon rants on, induces all the audience to lower their pants (*now* all those erections can be brought low), forces Sam himself into participation in his defiant game. Nixon has, as we have seen, challenged his two lovers simultaneously at Sing Sing ("I was all done with trying to outargue women, or men either, Uncle Sam included, to hell with respect" [436]), but it was a little phase of lunacy that passed quickly, privately. Now he is enacting that independence which is the mark of a nation or a man in the sites of passage. He had thought it out before he went to Ethel, thought it through in all its implications:

And so that was my handle. Exposure of the FBI in exchange for confessions, partnership in iconoclasm . . . could the people brook an attack on that faith? . . . if it worked I'd have them in the palm of my hand. They'd have to believe in something, and I'd be all they had left . . . Even Uncle Sam would have to toe the goddamned line! And it wasn't for myself I'd be doing this, and not even for the nation. Let's face it, the survival of the whole fucking world depended on us, and I was the only guy in the country who could make it work. (371)

He was right, of course; wrong in directing his fantasies toward Ethel, right in his sense of election. It has been some speech. But Sam, resigned to repetition, knows best: "'Okay, son,' he said, or seemed to say . . . 'Experience keeps a dear school, but fools as they say'll learn in no other.'" Now the goblins have come out looking like Sam (who fuses into Nixon's hard father, who watches from the front row). A clown, a blockhead, a bared ass in every sense, Nixon "stood rooted to the stage floor, petrified with terror and anticipation, my eyes glued helplessly on his strong pale hands as they pushed back his sky blue swallowtail coat, unhooked his braces and unbuttoned his fly, gripped the waistband . . . and then — BLACK-OUT!!" (485).

The next chapter, titled "Freedom's Holy Light," begins with variations on the theme of nighttime terror, which has pursued Nixon from those spooky hours in his office when he was falling in love: "THE PHANTOM'S KILLT UNCLE SAM!" (487). Dream time, Coover had said, citing Roger Caillois, "is a ritual return to the mythic roots of a group of people. A tribe might set aside a time every year to do this, most often during initiation rites — to take the young who are coming into the tribe as adults and deliver them into an experience in which they relive the experiences of the civilizing heroes."[28] And then, as Coover talks on, it becomes carnival in Bakhtin's terms: "If you go back to dream time, of course, you must first pretend that the tribe has not yet been civilized, that the rules you live by have not yet come into existence. So everything gets turned upside down."[29] What, though, if, as in Times Square, there is a place with no adults, what if "the light does not return, and in the ever deepening night-time of the people, the shapes of their fears are drawn from every deepening wells, . . . commingling now with shades of half-forgotten nightmares from all their childhoods" (488)?

Nixon's love fantasies of little Ethel, his representative self-election as the next incarnation, his defiance are all coming together at this circus: "'Oh, Dick, grow up,' Pat had snapped irritably . . . 'We're not playing anything, young lady, Your Daddy's leaving this room right now and you're going nighty-night! It's very late'" (523). Pat Nixon, rejecting and rejected lover had not only said this but also added, "You're going to give them bad dreams!" (523). He is breaking everything: Ethel, his daughter's doll, the rules; he is playing the dog again, the role he adapted to satisfy his mother, to be a man: "G-r-r-row-w-f-f! Beauty and the Beast, that game I used to play with Pat before we were married, my secret self" (173). We are back to the old fables and fairy tales of *Pricksongs & Descants*, and the tragedy of the burning and the humiliation of the Prince and the rape of Ethel are all laminated into a horror Nixon shares with the people, his indi-vidual nightmare a vertical version of the American horizon: "Grunt-ing and huffing, I'd lurched for the doll and tipped over a table full of games and building blocks . . . clutching Tiny. Now everybody was screaming. Because of the doll. Somehow I'd managed to take Tiny's head off. What was happening to me? I'd struggled for words, I'd wanted to tell Pat that she was the only one who could free me from this terrible enchantment" (523). He has been wrong about love throughout his life, of course; first Ethel, now Pat must serve him, save him. But he is getting closer to the enduring love, the bad old man who just will not quit when he finds one of his own kind. If the

28. Coover and McCaffrey, "Coover," 57.
29. Ibid.

recurrent nightmares echo those of an immature race, they are only the obverse of its dreams. As Sam impatiently awaited his arrival at the burning, he summarized Nixon's folly and endorsed his reign as King Carnival: "'C-r-e-a-t-i-o-n!' growls Uncle Sam. 'Nature never makes any blunders, when she makes a fool she means it!' He is irate, but oddly there is a frosty twinkle in his eye" (401). The true lovers are coming together, on an inevitable course that will unite the symbol Sam, the people, and the new Incarnation who shares so much with them both.

Let us return to Bakhtin to gather a sense of these emerging fusions that involve the private, psychic history of a little man with the Manifest Destiny felt by a nation, a "tribe," as Coover would have it. If their geographies are different, as different as their talents, both Bakhtin and Coover treat the novel as an instrument for anatomizing an antisociety and its symbols.

The Public Burning, like Richard Nixon at its center, moves along a broad linguistic scale from public rhetoric to profanity. Even being its narrative center, though, Nixon can never quite match the mercurial voices of Uncle Sam, no son quite catching more than a piece of this protean father and fast-talker, even one trained as, proving himself in Times Square as, a carnival barker. Sam and Nixon live in a place called America, which looks and sounds much like the dialogic novel it has become in Coover's hands: a place where linguistic and social levels juxtapose in strange choral counterpoints.

Nixon's America speaks in the mixed tongues of a classless congeries. But Sam is not fooled by the virtuosity of his own rhetorics when it comes to the point, which is racism ("I can . . . swaller niggers whole, raw or cooked, . . . whup my weight in wildcats and redcoats . . . and out-inscrutabullize the heathen Chinee" [7]) and — Nixon's dream and destiny — elitism ("God's glowin' Covenant" [7]). Speaking in the mixed tongues of the new society and the new novel, Sam and his would-be incarnation have pyramidal values. Bakhtin chose not to face the difficulties of dealing with this riptide of societal, of human, relations, preferring to talk about aesthetic, linguistic "heteroglossia." Rabelais was an easy choice, located at a mythic fulcrum between the folkloristic and the literary, and Dostoevsky offered a world almost equally unexamined (or one that did not demand examination): Both, after all, wrote about asocial monsters, giants and murderers, idiots savants and otherwise. These are classless figures or, to be more faithful, I think, to Bakhtin's instincts than his conclusions, people who speak outside the social landscape, *Auslanders*, occupying as they do that antigeneric territory that was born with the novel. Or, rather, the dialects that mingle when classes pretend to do so in "carnivalesque" periods:

> Every type of intentional hybrid is more or less dialogized. This means that the languages that are crossed in it relate to each other as do rejoinders in a dialogue; there is an argument between languages, an argument between styles of language. But it is not a dialogue in the narrative sense, nor in the abstract sense; rather it is a dialogue between points of view, each with its own concrete language that cannot be translated into the other. (*Dialogic*, 76)

When we arrive so late in the linguistic process as the novel, this *"heteroglossia"* will, of course, involve the incorporation of genres into the new antigeneric voice. *The Public Burning* incorporates not only the detective story, the (Greek) romance, and the public "travel" novel, but also converts *Time* magazine rhetoric into epic poems speaking for a nation, makes an operetta of the government's attempts to save the Rosenbergs by eliciting confessions (380–94), and a less moving version of the "dialogue" in which Ethel pleads with Eisenhower for mercy (247–54), not to forget the movie plot and ballad of *High Noon* (236–44) or the vaudeville farces incorporated into the Times Square festival, but anticipated by Nixon's clown act at Sing Sing before he goes on a national stage. What Bakhtin did not quite realize was how public and private could come into lacerating union at the edges of society, the edges we label carnivalesque ("in the rather common doubling by a circus clown of the serious and dangerous numbers of a program" [*Dialogic*, 79]). What Coover risks, and Bakhtin missed, are the relations between class and a different conception of roles, but a conception implicit in just these, Bakhtin's own words. Whatever our conclusions on Bakhtin's politics, or lack of them, he was inevitably conditioned by time and place in measuring the genre "novel" (a thing parading as new, as news, as history, at least someone's history) as an expression of a postfeudal, postclass society. He sees the inherent dilemma; Coover presents the novelist's solution.

The problem of noncollective consciousness is inauthenticity: "The motif of death comes to bear the sole meaning of 'morituri' [a fated end] . . . It does so . . . not in the collective laboring life of the social whole (where the link of death with the earth, the sun, with birth of new life, with the cradle and so forth was *authentic* and *real*). In the individual sealed-off consciousness, . . . death is only an end, and as such is deprived of any real and productive associations" (*Dialogic*, 216).

Coover's novel, the interlacing of Nixon's private and public loves as a repeated movement between plot and theme, or as, one might better say, the questioning of the American theme by the private plot, could have been written (as it was not) as a response to Bakhtin's romanticism about a space that seems never really to have existed in history between epic and romance before they came together: "Parallel to these individual life-sequences — above them, but *outside* of them — there is a time-sequence that is *historical*, serving as the channel for the life of the nation" (217). This is, of course, prenovelistic time, *epic* time, the time of heroes. And Nixon is no small winner in that area: He aspires to rule over a world raised to incalculable powers beyond that which Charlemagne controlled when he became protagonist in all those old stories. This is the world divided between the great protagonists, Sam and the Phantom, East and West, Light and Dark. We are back to mythologies, to that which Uncle Sam joined with Bakhtin in describing as "the national heroic past: . . . a world of 'beginnings' and 'peak times' in the national history, a world of fathers and of founders of families" (*Dialogic*, 13). And Bakhtin goes on to theorize that "in a patriarchal social structure the ruling class does, *in a certain sense*, belong to the world of 'fathers' and is thus separated from other classes by a distance that is almost epic. The epic incorporation of the contemporary hero into a world of ancestors and founders is a specific phenomenon that developed out of an epic tradition long since completed" (*Dialogic*, 15; italics mine). But it had not yet been wedded to the novel when Bakhtin wrote a pseudo-history; *The Public Burning* was yet to bring his theses about epic and romance to their fruition, fruition in Sam's self-doubling in the shadow of the goblin/Phantom, in the inherent Manicheism of the race that feels itself always "other":

War. This fundamentally historical theme — which has other motifs attached to it, such as conquest, political crimes and the deposing of pretenders, dynastic revolutions, the fall of kingdoms, the founding of new kingdoms, courts, executions and so forth — is interwoven with personal-life narratives of historical figures (with the central motif of love), but the two themes do not fuse. (*Dialogic*, 217)

What Coover has done is to fuse them, inviting the great American Horatio Alger figure, Gloomy Gus, into the epic where he wanders as a lost lover — until the founder, the foster father, merges with the biological one ("The person who caught my eye out there in the mob was my own father: he looked like someone had just hit him between the eyes . . . 'Hey, dat's my boy, over dere, doing dat!' laughed Uncle Sam coldly" [483]). This brings us back to Uncle Sam and the organization of *The Public Burning.*

Uncle Sam is ringmaster to Nixon's clown in the "literal" and metaphoric circus fantasies of *The Public Burning,* as has been variously pointed out. Indeed, he is executive officer in a circus that is perpetual.

Near the beginning the image is extended to the Senate to remind us that the Times Square show is big, but not a one-night stand. The infamous Joe McCarthy's press conference is described by an observer in unmistakeably relevant terms: "Jesus, it's a real fucking carnival down there, the whole place wired up with klieg lights and microphones"; Nixon, as liaison officer between the White House and the Senate, knows that he must keep this maverick fire-eater from "setting the whole house on fire" (55–56), knows that McCarthy is really only an extreme manifestation of the whole institution: "Each of these clowns lived in a world of his own, like a feudal baron . . . No wonder the Presidents always had trouble with the Senate" (58). *And* the Judicial; the Supreme Court had its independence, too, and Justice William O. Douglas exhibits it by giving the Rosenbergs a temporary stay of execution. But the ringmaster knows his role (at the moment of execution "Uncle Sam [is] cracking a mighty bullwhip like a ringmaster" [496]): "They have not reckoned with Uncle Sam's resourcefulness and his old-trouper determination that this show *will* go on" (68), and, summoning the Supreme Court into special session, he confronts Douglas: "'*What? What!!*' roars Uncle Sam, rearing up in anger. 'Listen, this is *my* circus, you old coot! And I'm gettin' goddamn sick and tired of you pretendin' to know better'n *me* what's right for this country'" (77). And the show does, of course, go on — in spite of Douglas, of Nixon's Sing Sing follies, of Ethel's clemency pleas, and of the world-wide demonstrations that the Phantom has arranged. The latter has even entered Times Square "like a cold unseasonal wind, tipping over police barricades, blowing holes in the set" (37); Sam knows it is the same wind that froze the thermometers at Ulysses S. Grant's second inauguration: "If we hadn't got one helluva dance revved up, he mighta turned the whole Tabernacle to ice crystals, shattered it with his twister, and blowed it clean off the face of the earth! No, son, you don't fuck with the Phantom!" (334–35). Among his Times Square blasphemies, this shadowy enemy has run the big electric logos set up for the show through innumerable revisions, until he settles finally on altering "AMERICA HOPE OF THE WORLD" to "AMERICA JOKE OF THE WORLD" (36–41). Sam is right: That is power, the Power of Darkness interfering even with Sam Slick's electric light show. But Sam can keep rearranging this wildly contingent and dangerous alternation of serio-comic juxtapositions with the master's hand. If Douglas's reprieve for the Rosenbergs has momentarily made "Uncle Sam, Judge Kaufman, Edgar Hoover . . . look like a bunch of clowns" (65), we have already heard him take back the show from Douglas. And, after the blasphemy, Sam returns to reset his advertisement for the circus of fire:

The electrical sign reading AMERICA JOKE OF THE WORLD begins once more to metamorphose, Uncle Sam accomplishing in three clean moves what it took the Phantom to do in sixteen dirty ones:

> AMERICA THE POKE OF THE WORLD
> AMERICA THE POPE OF THE WORLD
> AMERICA THE HOPE OF THE WORLD (65)

I draw attention to this small joke because it deals with an aspect of verbal dexterity unexpected from the tall tale, irreverent and torrential profanity, and Bible-thumping voice we come to associate with Uncle Sam, a voice alive with an excess of energy that belies the cold control of a figure who knows just who the phantom is, as does no other, and about the ever-present possibilities of mortality, which, nonetheless, can be forestalled or even transmuted by the carnival he is setting up to "reconsecrate" a nation in its Civil Religion. An ironic voice that knows the power of myth and the banality of its invention.

I earlier remarked that Coover has given himself no privileged voice of interpretation in *The Public Burning*. Nixon would want to be the interpretative voice putting together all these events, but the hope is incompatible with his role as a man stumbling through the confusions of his own personality, his desires and doubts about what his test is. There are no other candidates; *Time* as the Poet Laureate comes, by definition, only to praise the nation; the *New York Times*, the great Druidic Stonehenge, is a monument to the losing fight for clarity: It is Marshall McLuhan's newspaper as a collage of irrelevancies, "randomness as design. Design ironically revealing randomness" (190), until the readers "lose control. They twitch, lurch forward, jerk back, rush ahead, . . . panic and race recklessly through the sanctuary as though lost in a circus" (196). No, in *The Public Burning* there is no authorial voice, just "a text that would seem to have been written by the whole nation through all its history," as Coover said, "thousands of echoes, all the sounds of a nation." But, of course, such a text could come dangerously close to an extended version of the random design of the *New York Times*. And for all his insistence upon the primacy of juxtapositions, of "heteroglossia," Bakhtin realized this: "The author (as creator of the novelistic whole) cannot be found at any one of the novel's language levels: he is to be found at the center of organization where all levels intersect" (*Dialogic*, 48–49).

Coover is the author of *The Public Burning*, an intensely organized project. If *Moby Dick* is a tissue of Shakespearean plays and cetological texts all leading to epistemological doubts, Ahab has given it a straight line of quest: He will take them, us, to the whale, whatever that unholy grail is, in the end. Coover cannot do this because the quest and questioning are Nixon's part of the (his)tory, and what he is seeking is the meaning of just that history as something too large for him to either physically or conceptually put together. But if the reader is not to "panic and race recklessly . . . as though lost in a circus," he needs something more than Nixon's wavering plot line: He needs the assurance that apparent confusion is only a form of suspense that will be resolved by the ringmaster as authorial stand-in "at the center of organization where all levels intersect."

Let us suppose that, wearied with the postmodernist "entropy" view of where literature and society interconnect,[30] the author sets himself the problem of exploring this hypothesis: Energy is flux. But if such shifting energy is to evolve into the mores and mythology of a nation it must be reified into *metamorphosis*. If there is to be a spokesman, there must be a head. The body is only superficially the body politic, even the "people." In essence it is a sacramental body, participant and cannibalistic in its own holy rites of self-communion, self-sacrifice, self-renewal. Uncle Sam as author, priest, and executor of this Civil Religion is the head who tells us about it by simply organizing the babel of the people, tells them, as ventriloquist, this myth through which Coover's Nixon travels, which he strives against, succumbs to in the war between Uncle Sam and the "other," between the pattern and antipattern of myth and demystification.

Coover had talked about this struggle a long time before in the "prólogo" to *Pricksongs & Descants*, and had begun to examine its force for seduction and frustration as the Universal Baseball Association evolved from a table game into a mystery religion. In *The Public Burning* he gets down to a hard case, the American nation. It is a place where there may be not a falling off, but an excess, of energy, as Sam's hyperbolic speech and Superman physical antics warn — as does the public burning — of American apocalypse (91, 287).

But if Sam is our historical voice, and the Phantom is just a phantom — Nixon's goblin of the dark — a projection from ourselves, might he not resemble a wise-cracking Washington cabbie? This particular metamorphosis brings us back to Nixon's quest, not for love this time, or the Incarnation, but just for truth. The experience is a hard lesson; though Nixon is beginning to be inured to the demands of Sam, to dreams, fantasies, puzzles, he could not have been quite prepared to be so suddenly thrust into a clown scene become terrifying, because now the devil appears at High Noon as Nixon weaves out of Eisenhower's crowded White House grounds to catch a cab, stepping in some mounted policeman's mount's dung along the way.

30. John Barth's theme in "The Literature of Exhaustion" (*Atlantic* 220 [August 1967]: 29–34) was picked up by many critics but most thoroughly expanded early in Tony Tanner, *City of Words* (Oxford, 1970).

It is an ancient tradition, this, of the midnight/noon inversion of the demonic visitation, stretching back from the movie Eisenhower is reenacting through the fall of Milton's Eve to Saint Augustine and the desert fathers [31] (it is one of those parching summer lunch hours in Washington, an appropriate atmosphere under which the powers of darkness should seize the prime image of light's force, as Sam, countering, insists that the execution must come at the other end of the solstitial arc, just at sundown).

But this particular cabbie seems the ordinary cheeky item, who demands payment in advance, then "wrinkled his nose, sniffed, winced at me: 'Is that you makin' that smell, chief?'" Nixon answers: "I . . . I stepped in . . . something" (264). This expands into obscene jokes about Eisenhower, Churchill, Roosevelt, Truman, but Nixon keeps quiet, trying to loosen the filthy shoe that has somehow become trapped behind the front seat, sighing relievedly that the joke was not on him. Then it comes: "Say, I heard a good one about the Vice President," and the cabbie elaborates a shaggy dog tale until Nixon stops him, panics: *Don't you know who I am?*" But the cabbie, of course, does. And goes on to give an immense both true and fictional account of Nixon's wartime navy activities, not to his credit. Then the obscene jokes turn to Ethel Rosenberg, an epic account of her gangbanging the cabbie's neighborhood, and Nixon still trying to free the shoe and not realizing until "I glanced up in alarm. He was gazing at me, the grin gone, his eyes dark with a kind of weariness, a kind of resignation, as though . . . as though he knew too much" (273). "'Look,' he said, his voice mellowing, losing its hard twang, 'can't we get past all these worn-out rituals, these stupid fuckin' reflexes?' It wouldn't do any good to grab him, I knew. The ungraspable Phantom . . . 'They got nothin' to do with life, you know that, life's always new and changing so why fuck it up with all this shit about scapegoats, sacrifices, initiations, saturnalias — . . . ?'" (273). Well, Nixon is still trying to get his shoe free, with all the shit he has been walking around in, when the last quiet appeal comes (and who is the noonday devil now, that spirit of *acedia*, according to the desert fathers, which dries up charity?): "'Listen, it ain't too

31. A broad literature is summed up in Reinhard Kuhn, *The Demon of Noontide: Ennui in Western Literature* (Princeton, 1976); I discussed some aspects in a context that Coover might find less irrelevant than he once thought: *The Metaphoric Structure of "Paradise Lost"* (Baltimore, 1962), 130–33.

late, Nick, there's still time to turn back — forget this dumb circus, get on to something more — ' The shoe came loose!" (274), and Nixon flees to the laughter of those clowns who hang around the Senate.

The Phantom has challenged Nixon at this deepest level of concentration. He now suffers an inner conflict engendered by trying to reconcile his deeply felt sense of free will with the confidence that he is the predestined Incarnation (early on he projects Eisenhower's death, as he will project Ethel's love).[32] If he reconciles them at the end, after Sing Sing, he has already really done so in the middle of Friday afternoon. It is the self-meditation that is crucial to the private man's surrender to the public, but one that will need a lot of testing and retrying in the course of the day:

I couldn't take *any* chances, not now: I was waiting for the big one, and I couldn't risk blowing it. There are people who do not wish to surrender to the Incarnation, who do not wish to be possessed by Uncle Sam . . . who do not wish to feel his presence pushing out from behind their own features . . . the pressure in the skull, the cramp in the groin. Let me say right here that I was never one of them. It's true, sometimes I envied these people: they were free . . . [to] be emphatically inconsistent . . . To lead a land of free-enterprise entrepreneurs was to be their communal socialized possession. But this was what I wanted and so to that extent I was free: if these were chains, I chose them. (261–62)

But such a characterization could not have won over almost every public commentator from deeply negative reactions to the historical Nixon to a grudging affection for Coover's clown. Nor could the clown role, either, in itself: Pagliaccio was not loved, and Coover's Nixon is not only pitied. He would be, of course, if this shameless desire for the presidency, or his equally shameless desire for Ethel's love — if, in short, his indecisive love life — were founded on a baseless psychological greed. What brings him closer to us is the honesty of a philosopher who works his laboriously untutored way into skepticism about the gods — and still loves them.

From the first pages of the "Prologue," endorsed by the "Divine Hawthorne," it seemed that Nixon in these pretrial weeks could feel "everything tumbling irresistibly into place" (9). And Nixon's version

32. Page 29; cf. 59, 90, 116, 118, 225, 230, 261, 263; a number of these passages employ comic paranoia about Nixon's possible challengers to the succession, inserting another version of chance against myth into the structure of the novel and the psyche of its principal narrator.

is at first the calendar numerology that opens the coincidences of pattern we have already tasted as he works his own life into coordination with those of the Rosenbergs (53; 92: "June 21st was also Father's Day . . ." [his thirteenth wedding anniversary would then coincide with the Burning, but, speaking of wedding anniversaries,] "Their fourteenth! And what were *we* doing here on the seventh tee?"). When he comes to test the parallels between his own college days and those of Julius at CCNY, though, "by a chain of circumstances not all that different, one thing drifting into the next, carried along by a desire, much like theirs, to reach the heart of things, to participate in life deeply" (128), Nixon glimpses the irrelevance of pattern until *he* drifts into a deeper doubt:

Then what if, I wondered, there were no spy ring at all? What if all these characters *believed* there was and acted out their parts on this assumption, a whole courtroom full of fantasists . . . maybe, helplessly, they just dreamed it all up. Whereupon the Rosenbergs, thinking everybody was crazy, nevertheless fell for it, moving ineluctably into . . . roles. (135)

Nixon's enigmas at first merely broaden, as when he is working a crossword puzzle while being chauffeured through a traffic jam, and "suddenly saw the puzzle as a kind of matrix, a field of play which mirrored the structure of the newspaper and thus history itself, the paradigmatic range of 'news' and possibility, crossed with real 'time-arrow chain-of-events,' I felt like Alice lost on her chessboard" (206). He is, in fact, doing better than most *New York Times* readers until he leaps from the car, arrives at the White House gate just in time to comfort a beautiful child, then pushes him away in horror: "That haunting face: it belonged to Ethel Rosenberg" (210). He is right, of course, because it is the face of Ethel he has already incorporated from and into his dreams — "I *know* this child, I thought. As though from a dream, a beautiful dream" (210). Anniversary coincidences, numerology, and crosswords operate at one level. But when dream and reality begin to coordinate it is hard to hold onto the explanation of coincidence: "Randomness as design. Design ironically revealing randomness. Arbitrariness as a principle, allowing us to laugh at the tragic. As in dreams, there is an impressive amount of condensation on the one hand, elaboration on the other" (190).

But Nixon does hold on to coincidence all the way up to his rendezvous at Sing Sing, holds onto the private knowledge he has earned and recognizing just this — penultimately — as "my crisis: to accept what I already knew. That there was no author, no director, and the audience had no memories . . . perhaps there is not even a War between the Sons of Light and the Sons of Darkness! Perhaps we are all pretending" (362). There is, however, an ominous undertow, as always, when he admits that "I'd been rather amazed at myself, having thoughts like these." But he plunges on toward Ethel with the fullest emptying out of mythic content any Coover character has explicitly articulated: "Why be consistent if the universe wasn't." It is still a man on the edge between free will and socialized desire, between ego, the erotic, the erratic, and the political, yet the balance is tipping: "In a lawless universe, there was a certain power in consistency, of course — *but there was also power in disruption!* . . . And I'd understood at last the real meaning of the struggle against the Phantom: *it was a war against the lie of purpose!*" (363).

In his way, Nixon has become the Cooverian philosophic protagonist who embraces that anarchy we have earlier heard his author announce (and review) in the Nixon of "Gloomy Gus." But Nixon's approach to Ethel the Marxist martyr is about as likely of success as Gus's bomb run amidst the police: "We've both been victims of the same lie, Ethel! There *is* no purpose, there *are* no causes, all that's just stuff we make up to hold the goddamn world together" (346). We know the failure of result, the ultimate failure of conviction on Nixon's part. This discussion began with the question of Nixon's unexpected conscription of sympathy from so many readers, and I believe it has much to do with his thinking out this universal puzzlement. But he does leave doubt and Ethel behind to return to the embrace of his destined lover.

The Public Burning is a political fable as surely as "The Cat in the Hat for President" (later retitled *A Political Fable*) is a beast fable set in a merciless context. It is a context that brings us again to consideration of the notion of "metamorphosis."

Earlier I noted how Lucius and Pinocchio (not to speak of the trope's assorted progeny, which run from Bottom through Francis, the talking mule of the movies) had to become asses to see themselves in the mirror of a liberating "metaphor" that is narrated as though it were literal. Pinocchio enters the belly of the whale (the great Leviathan, image of the dark powers) as a necessary rite of transformation because it purifies his intentions. But in America, Disney and Disneyland seized upon this classic fable of a stick of wood's maturation into man and made it a commercial for children, then made it a machine in Disneyland. And Disneyland has come to Times Square, and Nixon, having exposed his ass before the American public, seeks refuge in the whale, is scolded there by his grandmother as a bad boy, only to have her metamorphose viciously into J. Edgar Hoover, that great, gray fairy who kept blackmail book on so many American presidents.

Pinocchio descends into the darkness to develop from puppet to man when he emerges; Nixon descends as a man and is reduced to a boy. After this experience, he goes home for one more try at finding a woman to love him — after all, Ethel is dead. So he turns again: Pat Nixon has coldly asked him about the motto written across his ass, has sent him woofing away as an abandoned dog (his old role): "'Pat!' . . . 'It's not what you think!' It had welled up in me: that new fondness I'd been feeling ever since the near-betrayal . . . I'd be nowhere without her, I knew. She was the only one I trusted, the only one I loved — I *needed* her" (523). He is an ass, and Pat has it confirmed by Ethel's message to that effect.

But in Coover's metaphoric (and narrative) economy it is not the symbolic beast, but the overlapping synonym for the anatomy, that has become literal — what Bakhtin labeled "the lower bodily stratum." One reason is reassuringly built into the party symbols of American politics: the Republican elephant is in the ascendant, but the ass belongs to the Democrats, whose "mascot donkey comes trailing behind [in Times Square], evidently excited by all this patriotic brouhaha and so bearing . . . a hard-on the size of Mickey Mantle's baseball bat" (457). Just as they come front and center, the elephant shits an immense puddle, which just *does not* hit the ass: Nixon, the Republican party, and the Supreme Court are all full of shit on this case (the latter do a long series of pratfalls, sliding through the elephant dung, all clowns, indeed [462–63]), the Democrats clean. It is a part of the American idiom, and so necessarily had to find its place in the novel, but also an important element in the idiom of carnival, of Rabelais: One hardly needed Bakhtin's reminder of "the defecation series" of Rabelaisian incidents, but it is a

reminder, nonetheless, of its need to find a voice in the relatively
chaste genre of the novel when he transfers his long discussion in
Rabelais and His World to the context of *The Dialogic Imagination*
(187–90).

However, much more central, decisive, to plot and to vision in
The Public Burning is the anus. Coover, could, of course, have
found his way around the Democratic donkey had he wanted to follow the fantastic metamorphic tradition of Apuleius and Collodi in
which his novel fits as "travel" novel, and initiation. But Lucius is
remetamorphosed and initiated into his new being by the goddess
Isis; Pinocchio, by the Blue Fairy. When Nixon collapses before his
supposed grandmother in the whale's belly, he finds the transvestite
homosexual J. Edgar Hoover. Pat has been an almost forgotten fantasy throughout the book, except as the woman who, a long time
ago, had tortured the immature Nixon throughout their engagement.
Ethel is separated from her husband in prison, is lewdly debased by
the Phantom cabbie's stories, and castrates strikebreakers in her
youth and a vice-president in her last hours. The prima donna of the
Times Square spectacle is the symbol of sexlessness, Betty Crocker.
In short, there are no women in Uncle Sam's America. One might
have thought that the Statue of Liberty, metamorphosed into foster-
ing mother, could have stood in some relationship to Sam, some
parallel or commentary on Nixon's search for love, but she is con-
spicuously inconspicuous. This, then, is a hard look at what has
given America a hard-on, the sources of truly erotic excitement, and
they turn out to be — well, before trying for formulae, let us reach
back for continuities. If the High Noon shoot out is one segment of
The Public Burning, it had already been developed as an antimythic
image in Coover's early play *The Kid*. In this western the beautiful
gunman hero enters the saloon, the belles surround him, then chorus
about his and their love life:

> Oh, that kid with Blue Eyes, he's ablastin away!
> Now, I've told yuh it's black with a little blue eye,
> But it's worse than that, boys, and I'll tell yuh why:
> It's also as cold as a stone on a tomb
> On a dead winter's night and it froze up muh womb!
> So, boys, here's the moral tuh my little story:

They's all kindsa fame and they's all kindsa glory,
But as fer my own, I tell yuh no lies:
I wisht I'd never been rode by the Kid with Blue Eyes! [33]

It gives one a little *frisson* to see Eisenhower come out on the White House balcony in the role of Gary Cooper, "tall, gentle, handsome, shy, his blue eyes twinkling" (243).

However, Eisenhower is only one of the incarnations; Sam is the inspiration, and, having always imagined incarnation, Nixon has always been curious as to its means. Nixon had as a young politician lunched with former president Herbert Hoover, a fellow California Quaker, "who, though shrunken, still emanates vestiges of that ancient power . . . We'd even got so close he'd confessed to me what it felt like that awful day in 1932, when he first felt the power going out of him. The strange hollowness, the painful deflation as his body closed in upon the void." Nixon, naturally, had "wanted to know everything, what the Incarnation felt like, how you knew when it had begun . . . He'd given me a strange look then . . . 'I'd rather not say, son'" (259–60). If Hoover had told him a little more, Nixon might have been encouraged beyond even his hubristic but confused hopes, because he remembers that from his school days as an actor playing Aeneas "they starting calling me 'Anus'" (50). There are the little jokes throughout, such as the one in Nixon's Friday morning dream of tomatoes (fruit-stand salesman that he had been in youth): "This seemed to justify an old proverb — at first it kept reading: There is no little enema" (180).

Nixon is an ass, but with the literal transposition of terms, he has been left open to experience or — if one is speaking of Civil Religions, one must employ religious terms, or those that can be interned in a theology — "inspiration." Every president of the United States is at one time or another trotted out as an avatar of Sam, and, like Hoover, a lot of them did not entirely relish the fate Nixon gropes toward through all the confusions of his sad love stories (there was, for instance, "that awful day when the transmutation did not quite come off and left only half of Wilson still working" [89]). But these have suffered through this being puffed up into a myth, into impersonality except as male impersonators of Uncle Sam. It is a role

33. *A Theological Position* (New York, 1972), 38.

Nixon has desired, and at the end abandoned (as he abandoned the quest in Sing Sing, as he abandoned his knowledge of the crazy split ends of epistemology).

He lies like a dog on the floor of his dog Checkers' room, hearing the eerie voice of Ethel Rosenberg's poems wafting through his window; but he is as oblivious to this (memory? resurrection?) as to all else that he has flattened into paranoia: It is one of the unexpected moments in the novel when, having seen her body swing into a fiery death, our romantic rebel responds: "Ah, tears, hurt: what did she know?" (521).

But, of course, she didn't know the dream of love which had made her only a phantom bride: "Ethel's aria had faded and in its place, somewhere in the distance, . . . I seemed to hear someone whistling . . . 'Happy Days Are Here Again!'" (530). He comes through the curtains. The macho father and all that killing come together into a terrible tenderness, which threatens the whole structure of Nixon's quest after distinctions, subdues him into his worst dream of power at his most powerless moment: "You been ee-LECK-ted!" (530). Sam quotes a phrase from Ethel's letters, and Nixon is shocked, but Sam gives the message: "I'se wicked I is," he replied, and Nixon finally understands at some level who the cabbie was, the whole way he has betrayed his dreams, all of those of those little boys who had gotten up to see the circus pitch its tents in the morning. Sam strokes him and says, "she's part of me now, both her and her brave engineer, just as much as Pocahontas, Billy the Kid, or Bambi — ," and Nixon's last whimper is *You're no better than the Phantom* . . . You've changed . . . You're not the same as when I was a boy" (531). Nixon tries once again to renege as the rape begins, but it is not in his nature to escape any preordained pattern: "'I don't want to!' I wailed in agony, twisting and pitching about. 'I quit!'" (532). But you cannot quit on your daddy or your daddy's dreams, so Sam screws him, and even in the process Nixon begins his metamorphosis, thinking, "this is not happening to me alone . . . but to the nation as well."[34] He's right. Recollections of *The Kid* interrupted me in midphrase a few pages back, and now I am in a position to

34. And now one recalls the Phantom cabbie's joke about why Mamie Eisenhower wants a divorce: "She's gettin' sick . . . of him doin' to the country all the time what he oughta be doin' to her!" (264).

complete it. What has excited America in Coover's compressed canvass of its history, its eroticism, is its perpetual embrace of the cold mad feary father, of origins that are never available unless the son invents himself. Again and again. If this world of masculine energy without women recalls and revalidates Leslie Fiedler's thesis about love and death, Coover complicates it immensely in two directions. First, we invent not only that "other" which is the father, but all that cannot be absorbed into it as the other "other" that is the Pan/Phantom of nightmare. Coover ironically and repeatedly invokes Horatio Alger in the course of Nixon's quest. It is, perhaps, quietly subterranean, the most subtle summary of the whole journey through the American psyche upon which *The Public Burning* takes us. Here is another old abuser of boys whose myth of success was peddled into the American dream about growing up. If one is wedded to a mass nightmare in which everything metamorphoses into something alien, somebody has to reassure us with a dream of self-love. Nixon always knew what he was seeking, of course, the power he wanted; he just did not know whether he could become what he desired. Now he has attained it, and like the imperial America that Sam and Coover chronicle, like all of us, at the nearly last moment his heroic questioning of mythologies returns: "Maybe the worst thing that can happen to you in this world is to get what you think you want." But as Coover had said a long time before, "The crucial beliefs of people are mythic in nature . . . To try to apply reason to such beliefs is like trying to solve a physics problem by psychoanalysis" (*First Person*, 152).

As Nixon becomes the Incarnation, he has to reembrace the American Myth of continuities, of fathers and sons who, because they are Doppelgängers, need no mothers. It is a tender comic ending to the tragic American novel:

"I mean it, Gus! You're my handsome carny barker, my wild Irish rocker-socker, my fellow travelin' salesman, my little accident, my pretty sailorboy!" He patted my bum affectionately. "You're my everything, sunshine — *you're my boy!*" (534)

It is just here that Nixon ceases to question his self-projected destiny: "His words warmed me and chilled me at the same time." But he accepts their identity and the romance quest ends at last: "Of course, he was an incorrigible huckster, a sweet-talking con artist . . . Whatever else he was, he was beautiful . . . the most beautiful thing in all the world. I was ready at last to do what I had never done before. '*I . . . I love you, Uncle Sam!*' I confessed."

These are Nixon's last words as he becomes the Incarnation. Sam's last words still echo in his ears as the last words of the first truly dialogic, perhaps the first truly American, novel. They are, I hope, Robert Coover's *plaudite* upon having been ringmaster to the most difficult circus stunt in the history of American literature:

Well, something attempted, something done, my boy, has earned a night's repose, so let the tent be struck. Vaya con Dios, my darklin', and remember . . . "always leave 'em laughin' as you say good-bye!" (534)

IV.

GERALD'S PARTY
Ars Memoriae

> There is, behind his ironic smile, a profound sadness, the
> fatalistic survivor's wistful acknowledgment that, in the
> end, the fundamental things apply. Time, going by, leaves
> nothing behind.
> — Robert Coover, "You Must Remember This"

"You Must Remember This"[1] stands in relation to *Gerald's Party*
much the way "Gloomy Gus of the Chicago Bears" stands in relation
to *The Public Burning*. It is a complicated and completely independent summary of themes and patterning, which Coover seemed to
need to look both backward and forward from the near completion
of the novel. *Gerald's Party* grew gradually through several years
and stages; just at the completion of the final version, he wrote the
short story. I say it looks forward and backward simultaneously,
because it reminds us of the novel that has been in the making since
before the gestation stages of *The Public Burning*, the history of
Lucky Pierre, a pornographic film star recalling his career. It also
thrusts into the foreground one of the cannibalizations of medium
(and now we are upon an intersecting border line with genres) which
Gerald's Party absorbs into the novel much more ambitiously than
did *The Public Burning*: that is, film.

"You Must Remember This" is related to the film *Casablanca* in
what Tzvetan Todorov (adapting Bakhtin) calls *superposition*. It is a
useful, because familiar, term to describe the interaction of two texts,
where the absent one is either parodied or stylized by the present
work. In "stylization," "the external text is not a simple model which
can be imitated or mocked, it provokes or modifies the present dis-

1. *Playboy* 32, no. 1 (January 1985): 122ff. (The epigraph is from p. 200.)

course."[2] But, inevitably, Coover proves the theorist as wrong as he is right: The short fiction parodies the romanticism and musical thematics of the original, while stylizing the dialogue (even, of course, repeating it at key points); beyond this, though, the story takes both approaches to the film medium itself, even while returning it to a state of purely verbal fiction.

Casablanca is not a casual choice. Made in 1942, it became synonymous with American film, with the cynical sentimentalism of the movies' second wave in America as they edged in plot (as well as in Humphrey Bogart's presence) into the *giallo* forms of suspense story: the Hammett/Chandler tradition of detective thriller, but serendipitously crossed with the spy story by the circumstances of the war years. And to suspense and the familiar protagonist, it added the sentimentalism of love lost to time, to those hard times of separation which the war visited not only upon Rick and Ilsa but also upon so many lovers in their audience. With the coming of television reruns, it has probably been viewed more often by more Americans (not to speak of its European audience; it does, after all, stand as an epic of anti-Nazi resistance by the French, by the Czechs) than any other film. And the endlessly significant, meaningless formula of lover's hello and goodbye, "Here's lookin' at you, kid," the theme song that threads the film, homonymic with the title of Coover's fiction, and the accompanying request to the pianist, "Play it again, Sam" — these have become evocative to numberless people who have never seen the film in its entirety, as Hamlet is evocative to those who have never seen or read Shakespeare. *Casablanca* is, in sum, not a movie but a myth, a myth complicated by the privileged, yet self-conscious, status of film as the heir apparent to the novel: It is the myth of the movies, the "dialogical" juxtapositions no longer primarily of viewpoint in any sense Bakhtin meant, but of form. The movie has become its own message, in the sense that the medium is itself almost never transparent, always threatening foregrounding. I recall a short story that kept turning up in popular magazines in the thirties and forties which consisted of a letter being typed in progressively degenerate form by a correspondent who was steadily drinking as he wrote. I remember it because, from Chaucer's palinode and blessing

---

2. Tzvetan Todorov, "How to Read," in *The Poetics of Prose*, trans. Richard Howard (Ithaca, 1977), 244–45. The essay dates from 1969.

upon his little book to date, there have been few written texts upon the physical aspects of writing. What is of immense importance to writers is of no interest to readers, as all writing done by whatever mechanical means since incunabula replaced manuscript turns up as mechanically anonymous: It is print, more or less uniform, by agreement detached from the author (we do not associate a fine press limited edition with its authorial origins in type or penciled scrawl).

Film, however, asserts the mechanics of making ever more urgently (the dream-work meshes of filming and remembering in Federico Fellini's *8½* being replaced a decade or so later by Peter O'Toole's rage at filmic tricksterism in *The Stunt Man*, with its hard-edged technicalities; as though we had moved from a film about filmmaking to a filmmaking without a film). And Coover is fascinated. I will not recite his flirtations with film, which have been recounted elsewhere. But I will recall some comments he made to an interviewer in 1979, at a time when both "Lucky Pierre" and *Gerald's Party* were in process:

I work with language because paper is cheaper than film stock. And because it's easier to work with a committee of one. But storytelling doesn't have to be done with words on a printed page, or even with spoken words: we all learned that as kids at our Saturday morning religious experience in the local ten-cent cinemas. Probably, if I had absolute freedom to do what I want, I'd prefer film . . . It's great immediacy: it grasps so much with such rapidity . . . And it has a relationship with time that is fascinating: we can take in centuries in an hour or two, even in a few minutes. All narratives play with time, but only film can truly juggle it.[3]

Well, perhaps. But perhaps, too, Coover rethought the problem in the next few years and decided not only that filmic techniques could be utilized by analogy in verbal techniques but also could be reabsorbed wholly into the verbal; the visual no longer being necessary to film. Decided, in short, to invert the apparent progress and make the techniques of a visual medium into mere adjuncts to storytelling, as Spenser had done successfully some time before in incorporating the vogue of Renaissance tapestries into the narrative of *The Faerie Queene*.

3. Robert Coover and Larry McCaffrey, "Robert Coover on His Own and Other Fictions," in *Novel vs. Fiction: The Contemporary Reformation*, ed. Jackson I. Cope and Geoffrey Green (Norman, Okla., 1981), 53.

"You Must Remember This" is a film seen at the beginning by an audience facing the screen as the projector starts up in the theater: "It is dark in Rick's apartment. Black leader dark, heavy and abstract, silent but for a faint hoarse crackle like a voiceless plaint, and brief as sleep" (but that "abstract," how did it emerge into this pre-framework of narrative if not by way of language rather than viewing?). The film begins as the wheezing leader runs out: "Rick opens the door and the light from the hall scissors in like a bellboy to open up space, deposit surfaces . . . he lights a small lamp (such a glow! the shadows retreat, *everything* retreats: Where are the walls?)" (122). And so it continues; it is *Casablanca* once again; but now Rick is watching Ilsa with us as the old film settles into sync: "There she is, facing him . . . the light flickering upon her white but determined face like static" (122). The soundtrack begins, no one having quite noticed as the familiar shadowplay began: "Their song seemed to be leaking into the room from somewhere out in the night, or perhaps it had been there all the time" (200). The screen is lit with pictures and sound, and now one is distracted into interpreted images, Rick and Ilsa seen, described, by some viewer, some director, and now it is Ilsa's turn to watch the movement as we watch her upon the screen: "Ilsa is staring off into space, a space which a moment ago Rick filled" (200). The airport beacon from the story laminates with the flickering light that disturbs images from the old film, old scratched celluloid and imperfect projectors, becomes a part of the rhythm of the history of their mutual self-rediscovery, their attempt to survive, revive the first encounter in the flatness of images, myths. For her, as on the screen with a matting, "He seems almost to recede. The cigarette disappears, the smoke" (200). It is an old movie, reliable in the way we know it on television, the song, the lines, the lip-snarl of Bogart (an old war wound he tells Ilsa; well we all know that is truly what it is), the comfort of repetition that we can internalize as a species of self-recognition. Genres, superpositions, stylization, old movies: We are at home.

Until with a sudden jolt we are, they are, displaced into another movie: "His mask of disdain falling away . . . he steps up behind her, clasping her breasts with both hands"; the old familiar film tries to return: "'The day you left Paris . . . !' she sobs, though she seems unsure of herself," as well she might, the phrase being inappropriate to the X-rated game usurping the screen, as "one of his hands is already down between her legs, the other inside her blouse"; with this action the old story, as well as the lovers, surrender to the new genre, and the dialogue becomes again appropriate: "'Holy shit!' he wheezes" (241). We are in familiar territory again as they do endless acrobatics with endless closeups of genitalia, one of those excruciatingly long and inevitably repetitive scenes viewed in porn movie houses. It is now that we realize that the *Casablanca* we have actually viewed at the beginning of Coover's projection is as sparse a story line leading into getting their clothes off as is usual in such films. (*We* have, of course, filled it in from the mythic progenitor, as we cannot in those other uncompleted pornographic films. Now the one we are watching has, with this thought, subsumed the original scene into itself, so that maybe we were never watching *Casablanca* at all, but only a plotless script to get these writhing bodies to work at play.) As we watch, we think back to *Spanking the Maid*, and recall that pornography can never have an end form, always beginning again the same limited, limitless maneuvers. So the names mean nothing, as maid and master are nameless in the novella. Yet, they did emerge in some now indeterminable fashion from *Casablanca*, where they exist as characters, and so these lovers struggle to hold onto the plot of their lives: "Even their identities seem to be dissolving; they have to whisper each other's names from time to time as though in recitative struggle against some ultimate enchantment from which there might be no return" (241).

But through all their moaning writhing, we have been realizing, with Ilsa, that the dialogue may have become appropriate, but that the soundtrack is not; it has relentlessly continued the sentimental title song ("Do you have a gramophone on, Richard?" [242]). She had asked a question appropriate to *Casablanca* when they first embraced, natural for the wife of a heroic man they both admire: "Is this . . . right?" (241). The lovers go for an intermission upon the bidet, and Coover reminds us forcefully that we are at an audience position of remove from the action ("He glances back over his shoulder apprehensively, as though to find some answer to his question staring him in the face — or what, from the rear, is passing for his face"). But now we are as disturbed as Rick (as Ilsa by the music) at the inappropriateness of her question returning in these flat circumstances as his question: "Listen, what did you mean . . . when you said, 'Is this right?'" The song says you must remember this, but that seems the hard thing now: She responds, "Oh, I don't know, darling. Yust a strange feeling; I don't exactly remember . . . Like things were happening too fast or something" (242).

From this point on there is increasing static created by the incongruity of the three films — the mythic *Casablanca* we remember, the abortive *Casablanca* we thought we were viewing at the opening of Coover's fiction, and the pornographic film the lovers try to reenter for another round of sex play. But worse, it is not only ourselves as audience who remember *Casablanca* but also the lovers; the new sex games are obligatory repetition, but they are simply acts detached from the act of memory, which each is exerting. Then the two things come together, as Rick savors the sight of Ilsa's perfect buttocks, remembering how often he has remembered them in the months of their separation:

As he reaches toward them . . . he seems to be crossing some strange threshold, as though passing from one medium into another. He senses the supple buoyancy of them bouncing back against his hand . . . yet, though flesh, they remain somehow immaterial . . . objects whose very presence is a kind of absence. (244)

If we think back to Red Riding Hood at the threshold of myth in "The Door," we realize the dimensions, confusions of Rick's struggle: what he is remembering is the future, what he is seeing is a filmic reproduction of the past, the present seeming to him "like a sequence of film frames. Time itself may be like that, he knows: not a ceaseless flow, but a rapid series of electrical leaps across tiny gaps between discontinuous bits" (244). He is right, of course, insofar as, like the immaterial buttocks, his present is as an image flattened onto a light-reflector, film time. But what is the medium into which he feels himself passing? Certainly not film, or even the pornographic film they are in; he has been here all the while before this disturbing self-consciousness. No, the threshold leads into something more frightening: "He is still thinking about time as a pulsing sequence of film frames and not so much about the frames, their useless dated content, as about the gaps between: infinitesimally small when looked at two-dimensionally, yet in their third dimension as deep and mysterious as the cosmos . . . and what if one were to slip *between* two of those frames . . . where would he be then?" (244). Perhaps one would be lost between the myth of heroic sentimentalism in *Casablanca* and the cutting-room floor of "Lucky Pierre," where that myth left all the sex action that is being shown in this porn extrapolation (Or is it really the memory that was repressed in the original film?).

Rick begins to try to return to the old plot with a sudden question about her desertion in Paris just before Ilsa is about to climax sexually. She objects hotly, and Rick agrees that it is not the right moment, but feels beyond this toward his situation: "It's almost as though two completely different places, two completely different times, are being forced to mesh, to intersect where no intersection is possible, causing a kind of warp in the universe" (246).[4] Ilsa, too, "feels herself falling as though through some rift in the universe (she cannot wait for him, and anyway, where she is going he cannot follow), out of time and matter into some wondrous radiance" (247). She climaxes in ecstasy, but she is right; like the immaterial buttocks, all of this is the reflected imagery from the film projector's light.

The discordant music from the film continues, "as time goes by." But it is more insistent, because Rick and Ilsa are now both struggling out of their pornographic film, struggling back toward the myth we remember them to be. And then we realize the "medium" into which Rick is crossing, the one from which Ilsa feels herself receding, the one we thought we brought to this fiction: It is memory. Articulated memory, not the repetitious ruttings we have watched. "She and Richard have been trying to tell each other stories; not very funny stories . . . but maybe not very true ones, either. Maybe memory itself is a kind of trick . . . Maybe the real world is too much for most people. Maybe making up stories is a way to keep them all from going insane" (247). In this case, then, we can redefine the medium into which they are passing from their discordant film world: It is memory as story, as storytelling, but now reconverted from light images into words. The song becomes more insistent; both lovers find they have lost their watches; Rick strides to look at the clock in the saloon below and finds all the characters from *Casablanca* gathered, silent and immobile, looking up at him, as J. Henry

4. This is a formulation that can remind us of the structure for that earliest of Coover's experiments in writing which absorbs visual media, "The Baby-Sitter" (*P&D*, 206–39). I offer some remarks on the story in "The Contemporary Reformation," in *Novel vs. Fiction*, ed. Cope and Green, 1–8.

Waugh had found the players when he returned home after the dreadful night of Damon Rutherford's death. "'They're just standing down there! Like they're waiting for something!' . . . 'They are not waiting for anything,' she says, as the realization comes to her. It is over" (248). He struggles, tries to rewind the film, as the theater begins to dim into that darkness in which we entered this fiction, "Listen, maybe if we started over . . . I mean, go back to where you came in, see — the letters of transit and all that." She knows the mechanics of repetition are an illusion; they can only tell another story — "We gotta get back in the goddamn world somehow" he says. But it would not work; it does not work. The projector light of memory is off, the room disappears ("I'll sort of lean here in the doorway and — *oof'* — shit! I think they moved it!"). Rick pleads for "that story you've been wanting to tell . . . And *then* . . . It's almost like I'm remembering this." But he cannot, they cannot, and he makes a final desperate plea for the complications of plot which *move* us: "Remember all those people downstairs! They're depending on us!" (249). And now we are subsumed into the dependency of being part of an audience that is internal to the myth we thought we stood outside of, sitting before the darkening screen, below the source of the projection room (249). In the darkness her last words float out, "'. . . I luff you . . .'" She has echoed Nixon's last words, too: "'I . . . I love you, Uncle Sam.'" Strike the tent, lower the lights, the show is over until someone comes along to tell another story, to trick us into sanity with another myth. And that one, too, will be a parody and a stylization and a cannibalization of another text, another genre, another medium, for how can we make things new except by an act of memory? But yet the storyteller, like Scheherezade, must always go on to the next stage raised by our "And then?" He must not — it is the title of a Nicholas Roeg thriller done occasional homage in *Gerald's Party* — look back (157).

The primal crime is memory. Let us explore this absurd exaggeration for the truth that it envelops, conceals, as clues are concealed at the site or removed from the site, of any crime of premeditation.

To remember is to insist upon a partial retention of experience; when we reify this around a person, the inevitable metaphor becomes dismemberment, a murder committed in the need for a talisman, a partial possession, of that which we can no longer possess. We then think of it as the embodiment of experience, but out of the corner of our eye we glimpse *disjecta membra* lying about, which reveal the crime of reduction which we have engaged in, a reduction not only of the subject now become object but also of our own experience. We place the self-murder of the body in time: As the good physician Jim of *Gerald's Party* says to drunken Charley Trainer (old athlete Choo-choo Train) going off, but also down, the track, that stuff is slow poison. As Charley replies, we are in no hurry. But memory is on a similar deadly tracking of the self as victim. We look back to a present always resident in one of those earlier time frames Rick had worried about ("A rapid series of electrical leaps across tiny gaps between discontinuous bits") because of "their useless dated content." Useless, because no longer present, and therefore dismembered in the dispersion necessary to memory once the gap is lept. But as we look back the poison spreads as surely, as slowly and imperceptibly, in the mind as in the body, at each leap of the gap diminishing the present and the past in a double murder. It is a little problem in what Inspector Pardew calls "holistic criminalistics," and in what Bakhtin called the epistemological destiny of the novel. Inevitably, then, the most sceptical of novelistic epistemologists arrived at the scene of the crime on the metaphoric vehicle of a detective novel.

About fifteen years ago, the collection of Coover's plays which goes under the title of *A Theological Position* was prelisted in *Books in Print* as *Murder: An Entertainment*. It was a false clue, a real-life example of those absurd false coincidences that stud the detective novel as genre. (And I suppose some avid collector is at this moment following that little piece of publisher's misinformation in search of the body behind the ghost.) this returns us to some early pages of this book in which we looked at Borges' detective fiction about a perfect crime based in mistakes, misinformation, a sort of epistemology come unanchored from its supposedly necessary ontological bearing. We might now notice what Borges later said about "Death and the Compass," explaining the relation between detection and dreams and the universal applicability, expandability, of their overlapping content, because *Gerald's Party* is a detective novel woven with dreams. The crime, Borges explained, occurs in a Buenos Aires of dreams: the twisted Rue de Toulon is the Paseo de Julio . . . After composing the narrative, I have come to consider the soundness of amplifying the time and space in which it occurs . . . the periods of time might be computed in years, perhaps in centuries; the first letter of the name might be spoken in Iceland; the second, in Mexico; the third in Hindustan.[5]

In its way, this is to repeat the truism that the primal crime is memory. As in dreams, so in — wherever they may have seemed to exist — memories. One is always looking back for the body that has become only a ghostly mistake, always (it is Bakhtin's identification of the genre of which detective fiction is metonymy) trying to find out. As in Borges' little speculation, a fiction upon a fiction, so in *Gerald's Party* the narrator is recalling a past spent in an improbable geography, but one remembered only with vagueness. The narrative genre and its tenor, the two modes of detection, fiction and memory, which refuse to be pried apart however much we pry into them, these are announced in the first two sentences: "None of us noticed the body at first . . . I was in the livingroom refilling drinks . . . recalling for some reason a girl I'd known long ago in some seaside town in Italy." But memory murders its perpetrator; it is not a form of suicide, coming as it does in the disguise of self restoration: "Yet, though no doubt I had succeeded, bed and unforgettable climax had been utterly forgotten — I couldn't even remember her face!" (*GP*, 7). The novel is studded with these free-falling lost recollections, playing between the romanticism *manquée* of *Casablanca* and the slapstick of the farce, which is also a major dimension of this deadly test of a suburban Everyman: "The mess in the hall seemed to be worsening . . . I was reminded of a similar occasion, stepping gingerly by moonlight through the wreckage of an ancient ruin somewhere in Europe, I was there with some woman, she was Czech, I think, though she said she was French" (90); "From our balcony we could hear mullahs in minarets singing the sun down: the setting, coming back to me now" (143); "I thought of teachers I'd had, bank managers, a doctor who treated me once for trenchmouth in Rouen" (121).

5. Jorge Luis Borges, *Ficciones*, ed. and trans. Anthony Kerrigan (New York, 1962), 105.

Gerald's Party, then, is a fantastic detective story about the fantasies created by memory or, to put it more generally, reconstruction. *The Public Burning* had been meticulously segmented; *Gerald's Party* is a breathless, unbroken run of overlapping sounds and events as observed by a single psyche, that of the narrator Gerald (no last name). The line breaks are a mechanism indicating nothing more than Gerald's movement from room to room, thresholds of the next locale of his psychic exploration. This structural shift imposed upon a meditation on memory suggests that one minor motive is Coover's salute and challenge to the contemporary author he most admires: Gabriel García Márquez. *One Hundred Years of Solitude* is, after all, an immense panorama of history turned to romance, as is *The Public Burning*, and it ends upon a variation of the theme we have been meditating, as its last protagonist finds the clue to the meaningless meaning of history: "Before reaching the final line . . . he had already understood that . . . the city of mirrors (or mirages) would be wiped out by the wind and exiled from the memory of men at the precise moment when Aureliano Babilonia would finish deciphering the parchments."[6] And in his essay on García Márquez, Coover focuses upon the craftsman's dilemma that the Colombian writer faced after creating his sprawling masterpiece, and the solution found in the unbroken meditation of the succeeding, and successful, *Autumn of the Patriarch*.[7]

In any case, the vehicular story of Coover's *yellow* is as simple as its laminations of genre are complex. As a detective novel, to adopt Todorov's distinction, it incorporates both the "curiosity" of the whodunit (from effect, Ros's murder, to cause), and the "suspense" of the thriller (from cause, Ros's murder, to effect).[8] This is true because the mad detective is in a cat-and-mouse game with the ever-guilty feelings of the innocent Gerald.

Gerald and his archetypical suburban wife (nameless throughout except as the "wife") are giving a cocktail party for the usual types: doctors, lawyers, insurance salesmen, painters, critics, actors; after the murder, a journalist naturally enters. "The body" discovered in the first line is that of the universally beloved, promiscuous blonde

---

6. *One Hundred Years of Solitude*, trans. Gregory Rabassa (1967; New York, 1971), 383.
7. "The Master's Voice," *American Review 26* (New York, 1977), 361–88.
8. "The Typology of Detective Fiction," in *The Poetics of Prose*, 42–52.

showgirl-actress Ros. She has been stabbed between her magnificent breasts and bubbles blood that soon surrealistically soaks into the clothing, the faces, of all present. She has been not only the occasional lover of Gerald and a host of others he is hosting at this party, but is remembered for the hugs she gives upon meeting — for five seconds she can give one identity and individualization as a spirit of extended love. She is also a dizzy blonde who has made more than one mistake, like that experienced by Gerald in his last dream vision of her: "Suddenly she grabbed my testicles . . . I screamed with pain . . . 'No, no, Ros!' I heard someone shout . . . 'That's "Grab up the *bells* and ring them"'" (316). This love queen is the focus of memory threaded throughout Gerald's evening, and envelope, first and last frame, of the novel. She is all wonderful surfaces, and therefore infinitely malleable to memory's fantasies. And there is Alison, the mysterious young woman Gerald has recently met at a theater performance (we must return to the theater) and around whom he has secretly planned the party. She is mysterious not because she is less openly inviting than Ros, but because throughout the evening she keeps slipping away, always a threshold never crossed, metamorphosing, accusing, a dream figure who bridges the fantastic reality and the real fantasies of this party ("'Hurry!' Alison whispered urgently behind me . . . but she was already gone, vanished like an apparition" [157]). And so she is a memory of a Zenonian future (and again we arrive at a crossroads with Borges) for Gerald. But if all fantasy for him, she is the "novelty act" (272) of some unseen orgy and the showgirl shill for a magic act of flags that unfurl from her anus in a closing dizzy carnival (293). Dreams of past and future, Ros and Alison are betrayers and betrayed by Gerald when measured against the reality of their existential earthiness; we have a strangely unattended tense for all of this gymnastics of fantasy built into the language: "might have been."

But there is a third woman inspirational of dream visions, and to know her we have to know the mad detective who turns the party into the scene of a whodunit, a search for clues, for — "truth." This is Inspector Nigel Pardew (also known as Captain). If Alison's exit as the girl in a magical ass act reminds us of the similarly murderous magic play with the female shill in "The Hat Act," Pardew raises (at first acquaintance) memories of another murder story from *Pricksongs & Descants*, "Panel Game." It is a television game show that costs the participant his life because he cannot readily work out the clues, even though knowing that he is in . . . "Jeopardy," that popular and torturous tease over which Don Pardo presided for a thousand and one American nights — or afternoons (a television juxtaposition works this in with a single line: "Bewitching . . . Pardon" [37]). But he brings other old acquaintances into ghostly attendance at the party, too, when he enters, "a tall moustachioed man in a checkered overcoat and grey fedora" (19), he has a pipe, an eternally misplaced white scarf, a puzzle himself as we, like Gerald, seek his identity (the avatar of power in Gerald's first view, if we associate him with Nixon's visitation at the end from Uncle Sam, both of their gazes "chilled and reassured" the needy observer simultaneously [PB, 534; GP, 19]). Perhaps it is the answer to a prayer for absolution: The "antique prie-dieu" is juxtaposed with the entrance of Pardew (22). But there is, of course, Sherlock Holmes (the surtout, the pipe) and Doctor Watson (his name is Nigel, presumably "Nigel Bruce," borrowed from all those old movies). But he is as inept as Clouseau fumbling through those films, "Inspector" Clouseau. But the white scarf — uniquitous, teasing, identifying — I cannot identify. This is the detective of all fictions, trapped in his epistemological occupation. In his professional capacity he questions, outlines Ros's corpse in chalk, probes under her skirt, dismembers, as it were, not only the body but also the memory of it for all her lovers. But this profession, like all madness, is also a dream. One that Gerald overhears unexpectedly as Pardew rests his head in the lap of Gerald's severe mother-in-law to tell of how (and now we perhaps hear the overt echo, homage to García Márquez) he had entered into the search, into detection: "'I'd always thought of that . . . as a parable on time — the hundred years compressed to a dream, the bastard birth of chronology, then our irrational fear of losing it'" (198). The mother-in-law somehow knows, and knows nothing, a psychiatrist who cradles the investigator not only into her lap but into his meditation: It is a story of a dream, but a marvelous account of the absurdity of evidence. The story begins at the beginning of Pardew's career, outside his dream; a parody of Borges, but also of all "detection." Pardew was called in upon a curious case (the infinite regressions of dream begin with the cast of characters: The first victim is "a famous historian — his field was actually prehistory, I believe: would that have made him a prehistorian?" [200]). Well, of course, what other species can there be in a search for origins? Solutions dissolve as suspect after suspect is murdered, until all the survivors are gathered "in the father's library, scene of the prior, and as it were, primal murder" (202). Young Pardew is brought there, analogously to young Nixon, and Gerald's mother-in-law comforts him in a manner withheld from the protagonist of *The Public Burning*, although he figured it out for himself: "'It was like a trial,' she said, 'You were being tested.'" (202). So he was, but the solution came, as to Nixon, "in a dream . . . 'A . . . a young woman . . .'" (203). Her name is truth, her function has been to tease the inspector into his rare ecstasies, and she has not only been his memory but also has borne to him the message of memory: "The victim is the killer!" (204). And given him his obsession: "What I want . . . is to *see time!*" (134).

Three muses, then, inhabit these men's dreams, memories. And in the present there is only the gradually desecrated corpse of Ros (the inspector does unspeakable, unspoken things with tweezers beneath her silvery skirts), the elusive image of Alison, and Ros's battered, shattered husband, Roger, who is hammered to death with croquet mallets by the inspector's loyal assistants, little Fred and crippled Bob, the uniformed Keystone Kops. Roger's crime has been that of being too berserk in his bereavement: He has looked back. But this makes the comic cops the instrument of destiny, agents of the inspector's mad dream of grappling Truth to his bosom through his art of "holistic criminalistics."

What is achieved is wholesale destruction. Ros's corpse dismembered in the investigation of its origins, Roger beaten to death, the morose-manic Yvonne, cancer victim, breaking a leg and being carted off screaming, the house a shambles, Patrick beaten, old Howard beaten (Patrick, a masochistic homosexual, loves it; Howard loses his spectacles and something else), Eileen beaten by her morose boyfriend, Vic (Gerald's best friend), who is shot into a slow, pseudo-philosophizing death by mistake, Tania the painter drowned in the tub, Quagg the director beaten, and so forth. And through it all (we are back to Bakhtin and carnivalesque inversions, scatology, to Nixon) Naomi shits herself in fright, and everyone has to clean her up while Dolph pops beer cans by the dozen, Vic bangs down the endlessly available bottles of bourbon, and the wife steps through this psychic and physical chaos with a Gargantuan hostessism ("'He's dead,' I shot back. 'Well,' she sighed, 'It's probably for the best.' She brought the bowl of whipped cream over and set it on the butcher-block" [272]; "Nothing was in its place, except perhaps my wife who was vacuuming the rug" [345]). This, in rough outline, is the sadistic thriller in which Gerald finds himself enmeshed, mugged, shot, puzzled. It entwines with Inspector Pardew's search for truth not only in his dream but also in the whodunit.

As we first begin to enter the story, this is sensed as the primary plot: a murder, a cast of dozens of characters, and all sorts of suspicious behavior on everyone's part. Simply to sample examples: "Louise stood up suddenly when I entered the kitchen, almost as though I'd caught her at something . . . she nearly took the buttons off the front of her dress trying to jump out of there" (42); "'She's been talking to the cops. I think she's naming names. I'd check it out if I were you.' He took Ginger's fallen kerchief from my hand, casually popped his false eyeball into it, and knotted it up" (53); "My wife came in with the cold cuts . . . 'It was the police,' I told her . . . She nodded. She seemed paler than usual and her hands were taut, the blue veins showing" (21). I mentioned the little nod I perceive toward Roeg's thriller movie *Don't Look Now*. It is about an English art historian whose daughter dies in an accidental drowning, wearing a red playsuit; later in Venice he seems pursued by a little ghost figure in red. Little Red Riding Hood to John Dillinger's lady friend, this figure of blood has laced the imagination. "Someone in red moved past . . . 'Wh-who . . . ?' It was the question, I knew, that had been quietly worming through us all" (17); "I saw something red, a dress probably, and a glimmer of flesh" (66); the inspector mutters about "the woman in red" (124) and later irrelevantly concludes, "'A *redhead*! Of *course* . . . !' Somehow she hit the landing on her feet . . . 'It should have been obvious to me!'" (184). It is *only* a redhead, the pigtailed and harmless Ginger. All leads are false leads, the murderer a grotesque dwarf who was not yet even present at the party when the murder was committed. In Roeg's movie the little figure in red is finally confronted: The lost child is also an exemplar of the adage that Truth offers Pardew in his dream: "The victim is the killer." She turns upon the art historian and, as she stabs him (blood soaks the cathedral as it has soaked Gerald's rooms), reveals herself as an ancient hag, a dwarf like the impossible killer in *Gerald's Party*. And this brings us back to memory and to the dream structure that envelops Coover's novel.

It is a party, a "wild" party in the tradition of the American theme and experience, as Gerald sees at the very beginning of our encounter: "People pressed close, parted, came together again, their movements fluid, almost hypnotic, as though . . . under some dreamy atavistic compulsion" (9). Dream can connote nightmare. In his one serious moment, the posing homosexual Patrick recounts the vision ("My wife said: 'It must have been a dream, don't you think, Gerald?'" [45]) that Ros's husband, Roger, had once recounted to him (we are always swimming backward on a tide of storytelling). Unconquerably jealous, Roger was conveniently placed in an asylum so that Ros could appear in a play. Then, one day at a later time, Roger returns home to find not Ros, but "there in her place, sitting in a chair by the window, was a strange old lady. Roger said the only word for her was 'hag.' An old hag. She had long scraggly white hair, wild piercing eyes a hunched back, . . . He said he felt a strange presentiment about her as though he were in the presence of some dreadful mystery" (44). As a character in a mystery novel or a dream, what could he have expected less than this encounter? The old woman accuses her son of having incarcerated her in a madhouse to gain her fortune: "Roger said he understood immediately that it was a parable she'd been speaking, one meant for him alone, *he* was the selfish son . . . when he looked up again the hag was gone. He ran to the door and found Ros, lying in a swoon in the corridor outside, her hair loose and wild, her clothes torn" (45). Blood guilt everywhere, and the time loops that memory takes in dreams trying to detect origins: "It was something about a fabulously wealthy old woman who presumably came to Roger with what was a kind of parable about love and jealousy, if I understood it correctly" (122). Michelle's dream of aging is closer to the center (the inspector has told Gerald about the case of the "West Indian omphaloclast" — "He actually cut them out and *ate* the bloody things" [132]): What happens is, of course, the recession of origins and the disappearance of their incarnations: "the worst thing about getting old . . . is what happens to your navel . . . It keeps getting deeper and deeper" (277). Michelle has learned this in the dream of an old woman, out of whose navel creatures crawled, and then she saw that they "were tiny people . . . And whenever they turned their heads and looked at me . . . They curled up like waterbugs and dropped off somewhere below . . . when I tried to see where the little things fell to . . . I discovered I was standing there all by myself" (278–79). The impossible necessity of memory and time: Michelle's is a sane version of the inspector's dream of time as truth.

But who is Michelle? She was Tania's model for the painting Gerald owns, a painting that he discovers, just at the moment of Michelle's recounting of her dream, has been stolen. It is *Susanna and the Elders*, but rendered in the self-reflexive isolation that is the paradox of this crowded novel, as it had been the paradox of Nixon's private/public being in *The Public Burning*, of J. Henry Waugh's loneliness in the crowded world of the Universal Baseball Association: "A gawky self-conscious girl stepping over a floating hand-mirror into a bottomless pit, gazing anxiously back over her shoulder at a dark forest crowding up on her — no elders to be seen, yet *something* is watching her" (38). Don't look back now. But everyone does. In another of Tania's paintings in Gerald's collection, a face has been scratched off: the model was Ros, the painting the *Ice Maiden*, Tania's self-retrospective: "The Ice Maiden — Tania — was swimming up toward the viewer . . . Behind her — below her — swirling up from the buried streets of her childhood . . . frozen images from her other paintings up to then — 'The Thief of Time,' 'The Dead Boy,' our 'Susanna'" (55).

Remembrancers, these paintings, stilled lives of Michelle, Ros, Tania. Stilled life created at the expense of some model now seen only as memory (Ros is dead, Tania is dead, and Michelle, Gerald observes, is getting no younger), and the play that put Ros into the center of theatrical fame had the same theme: *Lot's Wife*. Being the dumb blonde who could never learn her lines, only live, Ros, of course, played in a demystification: "a kind of dionysian version of the Bible story in which, after being turned into salt and abandoned by Lot, she was supposed to get set upon by ecstatic Sodomites, stripped, stroked, licked from top to bottom, and quite literally reimpregnated with life" (34). Vic, most sceptical of the trio of epistemologists (Gerald, Pardew, himself) trying to get at the heart of the party, interprets the play more cynically: "God saved Lot . . . so Lot afterwards could fuck his daughters, but he froze the wife for looking back. On the surface, that doesn't make a lot of sense. But the radical message of that legend is that incest, sodomy, betrayal and all that are not crimes — only turning back is: rigidified memory, attachment to the past" (187).

Gerald's Party is a novel made from the stuff of an abortive play, and it incorporates at its center everyone's memory (dismember-ment) of an actress who would not remember her lines. Ros was, in-evitably, an orphan, as were Ilsa and Rick; abandoned by the umbil-ical connection as Nixon felt himself in *The Public Burning,* as the children felt on their way to "The Gingerbread House." And we rear-rive at the primal crime that is trying to sort out origins. The navel recedes. Ros's womb has been probed for clues to her death. Like its tryout, "You Must Remember This," *Gerald's Party* stills things into language: "Language is the square hole we keep trying to jam the round peg of life into" (93). Tania the painter had observed this more caustically once: "I know we can't survive without it, Gerry, prob-ably we even need all those past and future fictions imbedded in the goddamn grammar — but art's great task is to reconcile us to the true *human* time of *the eternal present*" (146). Or distills them into all those photographs of the corpse which grow like empty clothing on lines stretched across Gerald's study: "Photos . . . did not preserve the past, they only distorted it. Memory, left alone, even as it purged and invented, was always right. Photography could only be de-fended, she felt (I understood this, recalling the collection of old postcards my grandmother used to let me play with as a child), as a fantastic art form" (113).

Paintings, photos, words, are all mediations into silence, little murders. But one remembers the absorption of the film into language as Coover's story incorporates *Casablanca.* So the other lively arts arrive to challenge language, storytelling, at *Gerald's Party.* The journalist arrives with his photographer to rearrange the scenic aspects of the crime; but, a minor practitioner of either verbal or photographic art, he is relegated to a pointless archetype from old plays, old films (*Front Page*). There are now only three realms of discourse in competition: television, theater, and memory. But the first two are symbiotic upon memory, as memory is itself symbiotic upon event without being able to recapitulate it. Here Coover is pushing fiction past Bakhtin's framework to absorb film (he had done that in "You Must Remember This") and the state of the art, television. But he is also taking these offspring back to their pro-genitor, theater.

Last things first, however — a simulcast: "There was a technician working behind the set, rigging up some kind of switcher between the cassette recorder on top, a lot of gear strewn around on the floor, and the screen" (172). It is a device that allows us, allows Gerald, to be inside the simultaneous actions that are occurring all over the house and spilling out into the garden behind, a medium that rationalizes the increasing disjunctiveness of events with the channel-switching technique that had become a verbalized form in Coover's fiction as early as "The Baby-Sitter" and recurs in *Gerald's Party*:

I caught fleeting glimpses there of the back of Jim's head, Noble doing an obscene handkerchief trick, Fats on the floor, the stopped-up toilet, Elstob yipping and snorting, Mee testing a razorblade across the palm of his hand, a patch on Sally Ann's fly that said "OPEN CAREFULLY AND INSERT TAB HERE," Horner with her, getting a message in his ear, someone's fist in a bowl of peanuts, bright lights, out of focus. (182)

The television is here, though, because this is a news event to be recorded, put into the tribal memory of mayhem, as was the burning of the Rosenbergs. We remember how the electrical machinery went wrong at that event, and it is recalled to us here: "Images were flickering intermittently on the screen, and sometimes in montage, as though the switching cables had somehow fused. 'Such commotions had a way of flarin' up at public executions in olden times — and recent ones, too,'" observes one character, and Inspector Pardew, too, seems to have read Coover's earlier novel: "I know. Contagious hysteroid reactions of this sort are typical wherever masses are assembled — it's an imitative ritualization of the bizarre and hallucinatory tendencies of the odd few, and always, I've noted, with a tinge of the burlesque" (182). This is one of dozens of allusions to the earlier works in Coover's canon. Within a single page a nymphet seductress metamorphoses from the girl in gold pants who finds the magic poker in *Pricksongs & Descants* ("She turned her back to me, pushed her bluejeans down, her little bikini pants getting dragged along with them," finds an ice-pick, "squatted to pick it up. 'It's so — so sexy!' she gasped, stroking it gently") to the maid in the novella who must be spanked ("the bed had been rumpled, the covers tossed back over it loosely. I lifted them: there was a bloodstain on the sheet, a small brown hole burned by a cigarette, coins, crumbs, a wet spot, and someone's false eyelashes" [79]). There are versions of Beauty and the Beast (90, 209, 247–48), and one-liners, as when Gerald realizes what Nixon learned before him, "that people are generally better off not getting what they think they want most in this world" (90). All of this is, of course, authorial amusement. If on a less programmatic scale than in Barth's *Letters*, the characters of Coover's former fictions come crowding into this already over-crowded party. There is a point to confusion, though, larger than the gesture toward the faithful reader of the corpus. With Rick, with Red Riding Hood, Gerald is passing the threshold between media in which time must have a stop: "It seemed to me, as I stepped over the threshold, that an age had passed" (163; "an age had passed, that much the door ajar had told her," *P&D*, 18). Perhaps confused by the television apparatus cluttering his story, Gerald, like Rick, thinks of this weird ritual they inhabit in film terms: "Change is an illusion of the human condition, . . . The passing images our senses delivered to us on our obligatory exploration of the space-time continuum, pieced together like film frames to create the fiction of movement and change, thereby inventing motive" (219). But this is a novel ab-sorbing television, film, as the cue words remind us ("fiction," "motive"), a novel that cannibalized an earlier Coover play. Canni-balized it, but also incorporated it into the dialogic patterns as a ver-sion of the inevitable carnivalesque, the circus. Gerald early prepares the way when he thinks, pushing from one room to another, that "maybe the last play in the world would be like this: an endless inter-mission" (181). Time without a stop, story without a plot form, a carnival detached from ritual because, Gerald thinks, "the trouble with ritual . . . is that it commits you to identifying the center" (97). And that is Pardew's commitment, his testing, as it was Nixon's in *The Public Burning*: "I'm interested in patterns. And the disruption of patterns. That's my job. I solve crimes" (126). Pardew is a regres-sive version of Nixon, though, one who is as insistent upon pattern as the earlier truth-seeker was intent upon randomness: "Holistic criminalistics *rejects* these narrow localized cause-and-effect fictions popularized by the media! Do you think that poor child in there died because of some arbitrary indeterminate and random act? Oh no, *nothing* in the *world* happens that way" (135). Truth, for the inspec-tor, is time, memory is the crime whose origins he is always probing, with ballistics, deduction, television, photographs. But theater is contingent, alive. Gerald knows it: "And I thought, captured once more by the illusion of pattern: What love shares with theater is the poetry of space" (110). Well, *Gerald's Party* is a love story, too. The older estranged couple, Dolph and Louise (the latter is the wife's best friend), are reconciled (301–2); the nubile youngsters, Anatole and Sally Ann, are engaged (297–98). These are preposterous endings, solutions as preposterous as that of the initial crime making the future in the image of a prepatterned past, a genre called — in the title of one of Coover's plays — *Love Scene*. It is a play about a stage director who cannot work up any enthusiasm in his lead lovers, no matter how many plots he trots out, from Adam and Eve to Napoleon and Josephine. He rants in helpless frustration from above the stage of this world of memories, as Zack Quagg rants at his actors in Gerald's house, at Gerald's party: "Wait a minute! *Wait* a minute! Let's get *serious!* This is *death* we're talking about, baby, *death!* — you know, the last fucking call, the deep end . . . come *on,* what does it make you *think* of?" (251). Murder, of course, and mimesis parodied as always by memory, and the circus of improvisation where even plot becomes an illusion as improbable and necessary as the clowns:

Even as they heaved the body onto the stretcher . . . Regina appeared in the doorway with her friends Zack Quagg, the playwright-director, and the actor Malcolm Mee, Quagg with his famous purple cape pulled on over a white unitard, Malcolm in faded bluejeans and a striped sailor shirt. Quagg was normal enough . . . but Mee always struck me as dangerously homicidal. Just the parts he tended to play maybe, but his cold glassy stare and the scar on his cheek always sent a chill down my spine. (141)

So Quagg/Fellini arrives with his theatrical circus to dramatize the demise of Ros (whose corpse he notices: "'What kinda two-bit tank show *is* this?' he cried, shoving the ambulance men aside. 'That's my *star!*'" [141]). Quagg, Mee, Regina, Vachel the dwarf, Hoo-Sin the Oriental meditationist/dancer, Steve the plumber, and whoever else happens to get in line set out a *commedia dell'arte* scenario of Ros's death, a little obscene ritual performed around her corpse, a little keening and improvising of props with an innocent child as author: "It hasn't got a name, though the kid's working on that. But it's about time and memory and lost illusions" (237). The drapes are down, Pardew is loose, Vic is dying, Ros is being mourned, and Zack wants the old *commedia* economy of words: "Here, we don't need every fucking 'i' dotted son — just give us the nub and a zinger or two and we can pong along on the rest" (237). Everyone is watching the imitation of life, and Zack explains to a neophyte: "'In theater, dialogue *is* action, man!' . . . what the play was all about. What had happened to that moment *in between*? 'I made up something off the top of my head about the proper height of altars, and luckily they accepted it'" (246). Bunky is repainted from red to blue, and we are caught up in this moment so alive, so different from memory that we feel ourselves at one with her when "'It's getting so confusing,' my wife murmured, . . . 'I don't even know a lot of these people'" (247).

It has been a return to dramatic origins (*Oedipus Rex* was, after all, about that at the beginning, that search for the beginning). Ritual and contingency always jostling us against a sense of ourselves. In *Gerald's Party* cynical Vic is the dramaturgical innocent who believes that "ritualized lives need ritualized forms of release. Parties were invented by priests, after all — just another power gimmick in the end!" (168). Dickie, hedonist and searcher into origins — he is the irresistible Don Juan who brings youth with him in all his young girl friends — knows better about a party: "For me, they're like solving a puzzle — I keep thinking each time I'll find just the little piece I'm looking for" (169).

But it is not a party, not a play. It is, as we began saying with Bakhtin's aid, a novel. Or, as we began further back with Coover's signposts, something older yet: "I could hear Anatole explaining excitedly that his play was really a kind of metaphysical fairytale, a poetic meditation on the death of beauty and on the beast of violence lurking in all love" (247–48).

Yes, a fairy tale, where Coover began, every experience reabsorbed out of its visual medium, its temporary genres back into the old form of words, the story of our lives.

The last line of the novel is for Beckett, for the way the fictional enterprise goes on. The ghost Ros has squeezed Gerald's balls, "'Get up!' I told myself. (But I couldn't even move.) . . . 'Gee, I'm sorry . . .' (But I *had* to!) 'Now c'mon, let's try that again! From the beginning!' No! *Now* — !" (316).

V.

A NIGHT AT THE MOVIES
In the Alien Emperor's Palace

A Night at the Movies is Coover's first collection of pieces since *Pricksongs & Descants*. It is also a novel plotted on the experience of attending that range of continuity enveloping discontinuity which used to constitute an actual night spent at the movies. There are in Coover's fiction the genres and subgenres of the old programs: adventure, in a Western shoot-out; a Chaplin bittersweet slapstick; the romance of Ilsa and Rick in Casablanca revisited. There are the previews, the serial, the travelogue, the short subjects, the cartoons, the musical. But there is also the important frame to all this nostalgia which is more nostalgic than all the rest: the theater, the movie palace itself. And within this frame another dimension that is either contained by the rest or itself the container that gives the rest its values (or, alternatively or alternately, both): the projectionist/viewer, the audience as fan(atic).

We witness reruns in *A Night at the Movies. After Lazarus* and *Charlie in the House of Rue* were published as limited-edition fine-press books in 1980; "Shootout at Gentry's Junction" (a laminated send up of *High Noon* crossed with *3:10 to Yuma*) appeared much earlier in *Evergreen Review* disguised as soft-core pornography, perhaps a first tryout for a play, *The Kid*; "The Dead Queen" and "You Must Remember This" are already old acquaintances in other contexts to anyone who has read this far. But all of this reworking is proper — submerged structure, one might insist, within an exploration of nostalgia and repetition — which are a long way from memory. If memory is dismemberment, a species of ritual cannibalism in the crowded scenes of *Gerald's Party*, nostalgia is a lonely act, a gathering back into new forms of the pieces of a past now accepted as explicitly mythic. We dream of our own old times through the myths, accompanied by a submerged soundtrack of old tunes, gunfire, bombs, labyrinths, falling, drowning, flying. It is another kind of memory that had been pulled together in the movies just about when Freud was dismembering it in theory. *A Night at the Movies* is Coover's Alice embarked in Wonderland: She makes up everything that makes her up. But that comes again to beginnings and mergers, to Red Riding Hood and thresholds, the "collapsing of boundaries." Coover puts his paradox this time as the experience of watching one(self) experiencing the alien:

"We are doomed, Professor! The planet is rushing madly toward Earth and no human power can stop it!" "Why are you telling me this?" asks the professor petulantly . . . there is already an evil emperor from outer space in his bathtub . . . [who] splashes water on the professor with his iron claw . . . "You're going to rust in there," grumbles the professor.

Science fiction in the generic sense has not invaded Coover's imagination even in *A Night at the Movies*, in spite of this opening. *The Iron Claw* was the cover title for a twenty-chapter movie serial of 1916 featuring Pearl White (most famous as the heroine of the more notorious *Perils of Pauline* — a heroine who is revived in the "Intermission" section of Coover's book as a modern teenager), a title that was stolen for an entirely different *Iron Claw* issued by Columbia Pictures in 1941.[1] I mention these because neither matters to Coover's movies except as a compelling titular existence: Neither has the alien emperor, who comes from a deeper source. Emperor and claw are interacting metaphors for a new epistemology whose cosmos is dubious. It is a return to the questions raised by Rick, by "what he likes to call his link-and-claw theory of time, though of course the theory is not his." Of course not: It is the projector in action, man as moving picture; but therefore unable to seize himself within or between the frames drawn ever onward into the reel by the mechanical claw: "There's always this unbridgeable distance between the eye and its object."

The *Iron Claw* is an important red-herring allusion because it supplies the crucial metaphor-within-the-metaphor of movies as life: the

1. John Stewart, *The Formidable Years, 1893–1919*, vol. 1 of *Filmarama* (Metuchen, N.J., 1975), 329; Ken Weiss and Ed Goodgold, *To Be Continued* (New York, 1972), 184–85.

iron claw, the ratchet, the link belt, the machinery that rewind, replay memories into myths. To seize its guidance toward the center of Coover's enterprise one must begin with the opening section, "The Phantom of the Movie Palace." Like Lon Chaney, he is a man of a thousand faces, none his own. And he is absolute emperor of a palace beyond the wildest dreams of movies' makers of alien space because he lives just here — in the old theater, in the silenced lobbies, labyrinths, the popcorn machines, the water fountains that will become nightmare Niagaras of his female alter-image at "Intermission"; in the tangle of film swept across the floor of the projection booth as he returns, "surrendering himself finally . . . to that great stream of image-activity that characterizes the mortal condition, recalling for some reason a film he once saw." The hand is faster than the eye: The claw forces us to see the repetitions of the face, of the old movies, of the old times that the imagined Cervantes of Coover's "prólogo" to *Pricksongs & Descants* tried to escape and the younger fictionalist tried to demystify.

There is a merger between the seer and the scenes: The projectionist panics at loneliness in the empty palace, enters the imagination of the Phantom of the Opera. He senses not only a lower labyrinth borrowed from that earlier classic version of the theater house as prison but also a screen and a screaming audience sprung from the films, from the deserted foyer, from himself. Projectionist and projected fuse into all this linkage of the claw as the projector, out of control, until we focus upon the projectionist who "can feel his body, as though penetrated by an alien from outer space." But one of the ghost films behind all this existential terror is that of the ingénue, perhaps Pauline, Pearl White, but certainly in peril; and the projectionist fuses again with this image to become the child-woman himself visiting the foyer at intermission and meeting the alien figure escaped from the screen into her mythology of men; he seems, as she says, "a real dreamboat."

Here we should review the sequence, the plot order that leads into this fusion of the two viewers and out beyond that moment back to *Casablanca* and "You Must Remember This," which supplies not only the conclusion but also the subtitle to *A Night at the Movies* (with a new imperative dimension suggesting the union of audience and film: One cannot avoid the menace inherent in nostalgia).

The opening section, "The Phantom of the Movie Palace," is itself subtitled "Previews of Coming Attractions," reflecting the packaging of film fare in the forties and fifties.[2] This is accurate enough superficially: The first paragraphs offer trailers from familiar genres exaggerated toward the grotesque: science fiction; a gangster in some raunchy version of *Guys and Dolls*; the husband-and-wife twin-bed romancing coyness of the MacArthur code; a dangerously titillating story of nuns and priests (but with a strange commentary, as if overheard from some professorial analysis: "The hidden agenda here is not so much religious expression as the filmic manipulation of ingenues"); a blood-and-horror axe murder. Somewhat later the projectionist, excited by his collection of old reels, Wurlitzer scores, and memorabilia, exalts: *"Adventure! . . . Comedy!* He is running through the grand foyer now . . . excitement unfolding in his chest like a crescendo of luminous titles, rolling credits — *Romance!"* These are the genres that the "Program" or table of contents lists for the three features on this extraordinarily common bill.

But as the opening sequence of trailers swings into the horror film, the audience herds toward the exit in mass panic: "They press their tear-streaked faces against the intractable doors, listening in horror to their own laughter and applause, rising now to fill the old majestic movie palace until their chests ache with it." And as suddenly as they have come, the previews sink away to nostalgia, the crowds disperse into phantoms: "Ah, well, those were the days, the projectionist thinks, changing reels in his empty palace. The age of gold . . . Now the doors are always open and no one enters. His films play to a silence so profound it is not even ghostly." This is the first return that Coover has essayed to the technique that made such a marvelous effect at the opening of *The Universal Baseball Association, Inc.*, when on a single page J. Henry Waugh hears the wild cries of triumph at high noon in Pioneer Park only moments before he rushes from his lonely room to forestall the late night closing of Diskin's Deli. In both cases, Coover invokes the combined bravado and terror of a man enmeshed with his own inventions. J. Henry Waugh is a rule-

---

2. Most of the allusive matrix of *A Night at the Movies* is adapted from films of these decades. The novel offers an encyclopedia of film reference, but the pleasures of source hunting (and, for Coover, of clue implantaion) must give way before the realization that generic lamination, not specific films, constitutes the main structure — what the projectionist calls "Purviews of Cunning Abstractions."

maker deserted by his universal association of paper creatures when he violates the rules through which they came to life. The projectionist is a member of this same class, avatar of a film universe that has become as evanescent, as alien to its creator as Henry's players became in the mythic stages of the league's history. He is reduced, after all, to the stuff he projected into the dreams of flickering light. Both men become rusting emperors trapped in their own wracked palaces. In a way, heroes who transcend Gerald's guilt or Inspector Pardew's doctrinaire ideology of epistemology. In a way, though, much more lost in the crowds that turn into merely themselves: The projectionist "longs for the least sign of another's presence . . . He feels like one of those visitors to an alien planet, stumbling through endless wastelands in the vain search for life's telltale scum. A cast-out orphan in pursuit of a lost inheritance. A detective without a clue, unable even to find a crime."

Throughout the rest of the projectionist's opening, previews are forgotten. Instead, all alien life having disappeared, the theater has become a museum of movement which refuses to be determined. The projectionist basks in collecting: reels and gels and links and claws. Chemicals and machines, processes of rusting, dust, running down — even the silver screen is full of holes that may be mere aging or — if kicked into form by a meaning-laden vandal — the straightforward message from a thousand-and-first face of the Phantom of the Opera: "BEWARE THE MIDNIGHT MAN! . . . As though time itself were branded."

Human life: Yes, that is the alien emperor always isolated in this palace of his own creation, his modern recreation palace (but haven't myths always been our funhouses, with their distorting mirrors?) in which he is reduced to a worship of his re-creation, of his silver calf on the screen. Yet the projectionist refuses to renounce control. If his projector tries to impale the psyche that made its images, the projectionist can amuse himself as illegitimately as J. Henry Waugh in his turn of dice, which turned mathematics into myth — but less self-consciously. He does not even know that his hope (he should have learned from the archetypical entrapped audience for his first previews) is mediated by his creature, the Phantom of the Opera: This is, in a parody that touches upon extravagances in filmic as well as literary criticism, "the stylistics of absence." It is, though, a critique as well as a parody: "In such a maze of probable improbability, the

hero can be sure of nothing except his own inconsolable desires and
his mad faith, as firm as it is burlesque, in the prevalence of secret
passages. There is always, somewhere, another door."

That is fear and hope. It is hope relayed from the projectionist's
original in *The Phantom of the Opera*. One can, one was told, oc-
cupy the palace, its underground labyrinths, its audience, its taste,
even its ingénue. It is fear because the phantom's projected image oc-
cupies the projectionist of the phantoms, a death-head image in-
vading the skull, the foyer, the labyrinths of another movie palace.
Or can it be another, if this is where every gesture—never mind
genre or mythic pregeneric hope—is reprojected for the audience it
has absorbed, a mass psyche rereduced to its moving *thanatopsis* of
the living dead?

The projectionist begins to live again, slowly, experimentally, a
modern Doctor Frankenstein. He at first thinks he has tricked or
troubled the link-and-claw machines, hearing metal moans as the
projectors tip and drip parts while he fiddles with two films simultaneously in the projection room. Then accidentally two films
merge, chemicals or chemistry bringing them together in a series of
sexual unions which are generic disjunctions: "A galloping cowboy
gets in the way of some slapstick comedians and, as the films
separate out, arrives at the shootout with custard on his face; or the
dying heroine, emerging from montage with a circus feature, finds
herself swinging by her stricken limbs from a trapeze, the arms of her
weeping lover in the other frame now hugging an elephant's leg."

A piecing together of genres: This is what the projectionist has
played at in his old palace overlooking a deserted empire. It has a
great view of the screen. But the old Opera House phantom was a
death-head. The projectionist begins to be projected toward the "exit"
the crowd had seemed to clog at the beginning of his imaginings (was
he alone in not knowing the power of myths?). He is immersed in an
old film about the French Revolution. In a crowd scene. In an old
movie palace. Moving toward the exit. The projectionist is puzzled
at this last of his projections: "'It's all in your mind,' he seems to hear
the usherette, ingenue whisper at the foot of the guillotine stairs, 'So
we're cutting it off.'"

They seem to do. But they seem to do something similar every
week, so that the latest chapter in the "serial" follows the previews:
An Eastern thriller from the Bible, "After Lazarus" is wholly a crea-

tion of the projector. No one speaks, the corpse is seen, the priest is seen, the dusty village streets are seen through the crazed, discordant angles of the hand-held (primitive times, primitive techniques) lens as it follows corpse, mourners, priest to a window, to a cloth-shuttered door, to the grave. A movie, then, of somewhere in the Near East: But why not the "travelogue"? Because the priest, the mourners, the lost one are a single presence, each face a mask of the other. One begins a movement toward the sexual mergers of the "Intermission": the "serial" is person, not action: "he or she reveals a face identical to that of the priest, the pallbearers, dead man, etc." Should one follow the camera along the wavering village streets, or the myth structured along biblical lines? Or, having done both in the course of projection, must one accept the end of moving pictures at their beginning in silent film, wordless icons of ourselves: "The priest nods, the pallbearers lower the casket toward the camera. Sudden blackness, the murmur ceasing abruptly. Silence. Then, in the darkness, a faint nearby scraping sound, . . . Silence. Again the scraping, louder. Silence. Again the scraping, faint again. Silence." Everything mirrors, repetitions of self less exciting than those that rouse the projectionist (but this serial, too, is a mere element in his progressive concern with the meaning of the moving picture).

We arrive at the first of the feature films, an adventure Western, and one begins to become nervous about suspense (in the "serial" nothing follows). One becomes nervous about the autonomy of filmic style: In this lamination of Glenn Ford and Gary Cooper, the Mexican bandido speaks with a bilingual eloquence that absorbs into its virtuosity all potential interest in the contributing genres. It is the historian's opportunity to point to sources, but the alien's turn to return Wallace Beery's dubious compliment to Pancho Villa in a down and dirty movie triumph that suggests the jester will return eternally while the Lazarus lies scratching underground. The serial that seems ended phases into a more continuous myth. But wait; what continues? Not resurrection or restructuring of old faces. Just death. Unafraid, the Mexican cowboy sits on a pail, tricks the sheriff, shoots for tomorrow. A silver bullet pierces the myth. But this is only a night at the movies. What comes next? The "short subjects": unhappy limits we live with, a dream framing we only imagine we invent. But our dreams are grand, "Gilda's Dream"; our limits are real, even if imagined "inside the frame," a pedagogical device, the "iron claw" that sets limits.

"Gilda" is a very foreshortened dream, even with the interpretations of a critic who has been to the movies. There is no difficulty for him in following the dream's bases in the film: The dreamer is in Buenos Aires; the languages are mixed; the striptease is central. And in that fine fusion that relates the structuring of dream and film, the protagonist Glenn Ford carries over from *3:10 to Yuma* into his other vehicle *Gilda*. But he is also Gilda, a merger carried out in a men's room that is metonymy for the whole movie palace: "Well, it was a washroom, there were probably mirrors." He/she is ogled through the next stall (in the previews the priest had catechized the nun in such a place; home of the "holey altar," the teen-age ingénue will say in another metamorphosis). Coover is pressing beyond the great fart-master Don Pedo of the "Shootout" ("The Mexican bandit he is famoso for many talents, but none has attracted more notices than that for which his dear mama bruja named him") back toward Nixon's frustrations in a taxi piloted by yet another alien. It is Bakhtin's "lower bodily stratum" become an image of the images we live by, all that ingested stuff we do not accept as self: "I was breaking into little pieces, and not all of them seemed to be my own . . . so I understood that the fear in the room belonged to the room itself and not to me . . . I was back together again! But then I heard the click of the secret weapon [the "link-and-claw" theory in action], realized that my surrender . . . had disturbed the categories." Gilda's categories here, of course, came from her film and dictated its ending: suicide as murder, or the by now old routine in the alien movie palace. But this time it is not the projectionist (or audience) who attempts to become the artist of escape, but the archetype itself who, then, in the ensuing segment dodges into anonymity. We are learning that if the previews of the projectionist can abort plot, so can the projected imaginations when turned loose into their own filmic, non-Freudian dreams.

They are literally filmic, the title of the next short being "Inside the Frame." But the frame takes on the habit of dreams when it extends its literalness into another field of discourse: the house in a tumble-weed-strewn "street, lined by low ramshackle wooden buildings. A loosely hinged screen door [the ubiquity of film terms in our language] bangs repetitiously . . . a young woman opens a door and peers out, framed by the darkness within." Gilda's dream was born of the details from her screen life. But the dream here (another little murder — they crop up everywhere in *A Night at the Movies* as they did at *Gerald's Party*: "The door of the bus opens and two men step down. After a brief discussion, one of them shoots the other") is a group dream engendered by the movies en masse: Everybody's adventure is the profferal of ominous anonymity. Sources are not to be found; they are the forms before beginnings.

The sound of a cash register suggests a purchase. In the distance, a riderless horse can be seen, its flanks trembling and glistening with sweat. More martial music [this is the first we have heard], steadily approaching. The figure on the roof is an Indian. A tall man is holding a limp woman in his arms before a window. A couple swirl past, arms linked, singing at the tops of their voices. There is something startling about this.

What is startling is the specific lack of specificity: We have all been here, where these things are happening in their careful disorder, at no movie, just the movies. We are inside their frames even in dreams — it has all happened before, and before we begin to watch. Perhaps if we need desperately to grasp at beginnings, try to think out origins, they might take us again along the distance from film back to tale, to Red Riding Hood at granny's door, the young girl already knowing "pricksongs" through a rhythm as archetypal as a heartbeat: "What occurs between them is partly hidden . . . as though to suggest in this display the terrible vulnerability of thresholds." Or, perhaps, with the interpretive query as we try to awaken from this universal dream, we stand once again before the Gingerbread House. Another dream palace, old place. But a dog is dying, the rain pounds. "And the banging door? The banging door?"

Never mind: on with the circus. The second feature of the night (COMEDY!) is a homage to the bittersweet of Chaplin — "Charlie in the House of Rue" — another dream sequence stitched from the *lazzi* of his movies. And at the head of the staircase, among the fallen roses, magnet to the sprawling clown, is the recurrent ingénue introduced in the projectionist's coming attractions: She has emerged in the full-length feature at last. Beginning finally, how long can it last: "Unexpectedly, she reaches out dolefully and touches his face — he ducks his head shyly, steps back, and finds himself somersaulting backwards down the stairs." Everything rearranges into a library of light, a projection room that might be a diabolical version of J. Henry Waugh's cubicle in Zifferblatt's office suite: Charlie is confronted with "the blank faces of the room's multitudinous clocks." Time is so important in this inner world of repetition because of its absence; if only one might count on the Mex to arrive at 12:10 or upon the regularity of railroads into and out of reality: "The 5:40 to Churley is already pulling out of the Number 4 platform across the way and the Ketchworth train, due to depart at 5:43, is arriving on platform Number 3." But one can count on nothing in dreams: Having met the silence of an "old man," Charlie sees him "receding like a leave-taker on a train platform, Charlie rising to his feet and waving his wet cigar at him in befuddled farewell." Murders multiply as Charlie grasps at the hanged ingénue's feet to inadvertently finish her, and stares about at the end not into time but space — or the failure of either to substantiate the myth that seems to be playing out badly: "He can see nothing below him — nor above him: the balustrade too has vanished into the deepening shadows, the darkness irising in on him like the onset of blindness." If this is comedy, Pagliaccio weeps: "He clings to her, pants adroop, tears in his eyes . . . gazing into the encircling gloom with a look of anguish and bewilderment, as though to ask: What kind of place is this? Who took the light away? And why is everybody laughing?" It is the sort of puzzlement Rick will feel too as the film winds down to a nonconclusion, reducing his dreams, himself to a final few flickering reflections.

But before Rick and Elsa can return in another context, before Charlie tumbles through this second feature, we have another movie about ourselves at the movies. "Milford Junction, 1939: A Brief Encounter," because it is labeled a "travelogue," may be the segment most puzzling to readers too young to have squirmed through Lowell Thomas's soporific Arabian deserts and Incan pyramids. The genre was a teaser between the serials and the seeming seriousness of the main features. They offered a slow education inappropriately conducted in the palace which promised delight. Coover co-opts this reaction in a double reenactment, an inner commentary, as it were, upon A Night at the Movies. The "travelogue" is not a parody of that forgotten form, not an imitation, but the closest re-creation in the collection of a specific movie, the Noel Coward classic, Brief En-

counter. It is generically displaced, though, because it is an examination of the place where all the parasitic myths merge: the projectionist's darkening place, our alien movie palace.

"Milford Junction" is a pointillist tapestry of details from the original screenplay and its imagery: The train swoops upon the platform, which is entrance to this place of excitement; the cinder in the eye becomes a blinding danger; Mr. Godby reigns over the tea shop of "refreshments"; the assignations are made: "Next Thursday! Yes, next Thursday!" Unlike its original, though, this is not a travelogue into the little psychic space of the timid lovers. It is not really "all perfectly ordinary perhaps to those who live here, but quite thrilling, you know, if you're from some place like Churley or Ketchworth. Milford: it's like a magical storybook place." A bit more exciting, perhaps, than David Lean knew as he directed the film a half-century earlier, just as *Casablanca* picks up some steaminess under Coover's redirection. At least, the lovers fumble and fuck in the refreshment room, breaking the mores of marriage and movies remarked upon in the previews ("The husband and wife, in response to some code from the dreamtime of the race, crawl into separate beds"). But Milford Junction has more than this updating to recommend it as the magical storybook place. It is the site of the movie not only about alien intrusions ("The citizens of Milford do not really think of the station at Milford Junction as part of their town at all, but rather as a sort of outer gate through which flow all the people who come here from the villages around, drawn to the bustling High Street with its chemists, gift shops, cafes, cinemas") but also about essence. This is quiet Everyman's Everyplace, the locus (finally we have established it) of the movie palace. Audience, projector, and projected plot have come together as a place as placid as a hometown housing the hidden horrors of the palace (another merger):

At night all this vanishes and there is only the Milford Junction railway station. It's almost as though the citizens of Milford might be mistaken: as though the market town of which they're so proud might be little more than a theatrical performance put on each day for the customers giving up their tickets on arrival at the Milford Junction Station barrier, then folding up each night as the customers return, a setting as ephemeral, as phantasmal as those of the afternoon pictures down at the Palladium or the Palace.

Everyone comes here to see themselves coming or going from the light: The train "platforms already beginning to slide away into the night like the last of the rolling titles in a picture show at the Palladium, the shadowy figures on the platforms now little more than some nameless creatures who have no reality at all and who soon vanish altogether, the accelerating landscape, framed by the train window, gradually receding into a kind of distant panoramic backdrop for one's own dreams and memories, projected onto the strange blurry space inbetween, which is more or less where the window is, but is not the window itself." Now we arrive at the rationale for "Milford Junction's" specificity of allusion following upon the archetypal, nonspecific allusiveness of "Inside the Frame," arrive at the rationale for Coover's displacement of its genre: "It's like a magical storybook place, just waiting to be filled up, to be, for one wildly happy moment (though it can't last of course, nothing lasts, really) *inhabited* . . . It's like watching the pictures and being *in* them at the same time."

The link-and-claw inexorably repeat ourselves; the projectionist knew that if he was haunted by aliens they were versions of self. He inhabited their origins. Myths begin in the Palace of Wisdom. First we dreamed it, then we filmed it: The endless push-pull, reruns, returns upon ourselves when we find to our surprise that we inhabit the alien, too.

As there is an "inbetween" space linked by the claw, so there is an intermission in cohabitation with ourselves, while the projectionist rewinds the reels. He has pursued the ingénue in various guises right to the surrealistic shambles in which Charlie ends his dream visit to the house of rue. Now the lights go on and she emerges into the lobby, a youth revivifying the popcorn machines, the candy counters of this foyer that had become so ghostly (no: beyond that imaginable limit he had said) to the projectionist who pursued himself in her. The silence is broken; the place is all inhabited again as she sees the alien looking (nothing surprises now in the way of metamorphoses) like Rick: "He smiles faintly, blows smoke, then holds up the pack." She is gathered out of this dream by gangsters, a car chase, a fall over Niagara Falls, a little jungle scene, a turn back into the old Valentino movies she can't remember, but does: "She's his new favorite and is to be his bride. Tonight. Of course, there are a lot of brides, the palace is full of veiled ladies sneaking about." Of course, as she remarks: We have seen and loved them all. And yet tried to flee the palace. But our flight has been recorded on film and memory:

She pulls, punches, twists, kicks, flicks, slaps, and screams at every dobob on the panel . . . but nothing works, so she finally just closes her eyes, hugs the steering gidget between her legs (maybe she's thinking about one of the old chewed-up dolls she still sleeps with on lonely nights,) . . . and shrinks back from the impending blow. Which doesn't come. She opens her eyes to find the old clattertrap miraculously rattling straight up into the moonlit sky, the palace and then the oasis disappearing into the darkness beneath her . . . She's diving straight back to where she came from.

She returns just to the place whence she arose to enter the lobby. The cartoons are on a violence binge, her girlfriend has died sucking cock on a cowboy who found his image in the movies, and she/he, ingénue and projectionist, have finally succumbed to myths as (it is a little reminder) Nixon did before them: "Like her friend would say, if she were still alive: 'Sometimes, sweetie, you just have to hunker down, spread your cheeks, and let nature take its curse.' Anyway, as far as she can tell, the claw only wants her to watch the movie, and, hey, she's been watching movies all her life, so why stop now, right? Besides, isn't there always a happy ending?"

"It comes," she believes, "with the price of the ticket." Well, not always. There is a musical interlude adapted from *Top Hat*, which Coover presents as another murder film, a striking down of the avatars of an alien Fred Astaire (we are back to "Lazarus," but by now we know it is *all* a serial), another displacement of genres. But only as preparation for the final feature, for Rick and Elsa's interlude. The lights flicker across the street, across the screen. "You Must Remember This" becomes an imperative again, this time a structural imperative, to liberate Coover's epistemologists and storytellers into Rick's puzzle about their source. Old and young, there is a lot of remembering, and little of it our own.

This is what Coover has written about, committed himself to, for these decades. "You Must Remember This" is a rethinking, doubling back, a möbius strip of the evanescent become the inevitable. A young girl at the door. Some father farther outside, but still within the myth. And aren't they one and the same, really? Film, forever the sameness because the plot can't advance without the old claw ("I couldn't even move"). "But," like all storytellers, he remembers, "I *had* to." From all the contexts Coover has ever engaged, the last words always seem the same beginning: "'Now c'mon, let's try that again!'" We said that before

INDEX

INDEX

Coover, Robert, works by *(continued)*
dent," 36n; "Prólogo," 7–8, 11, 39,
50, 59, 103, 138; "The Romance of
the Thin Man and the Fat Lady,"
69n); *The Public Burning*, 2, 16, 18,
26, 34, 49, 57, 58, 59–67 passim,
67–113, 114, 121, 124, 126, 127,
130, 131, 132, 133, 143, 148; "The
Reunion," 23n; "Soccer as an
Existential Sacrament," 35; *Spanking
the Maid*, 55–58, 118, 132; "That
F'kucken Karl Marx," 65n; *A
Theological Position*, 24–25, 122
("The Kid," 71, 109–10, 136; "Love
Scene," 134; "A Theological Position," 24–25); *The Universal Baseball
Association, Inc., J. Henry Waugh,
Prop.*, 26, 28, 34, 35–53, 56, 58, 64,
70, 76, 88, 103, 120–21, 130, 139,
140, 145
Coward, Noel, 145–46
Creator, disappearance of, 24, 40–42,
46–51, 71–72, 102, 120–21, 140

Damon and Pythias, 52
Devil. *See* Noonday devil
Disney, Walt, 16, 68, 108
Dostoevsky, Fyodor, 73–76, 80, 97
Dream, 49, 69–70, 74, 90–93, 106,
122–23, 126–27, 129–30, 142–45, 147
Durkheim, Emile, 69

Eisenhower, Dwight D., 85

Fables, 9, 25–34
Fairy tales, 9–19, 135
Faulkner, William, 21
Fellini, Federico, 116, 134
Fiedler, Leslie, 112
Film. *See* Genre theory
Flaubert, Gustave, 2
Ford, Glenn, 142, 143
Freud, Sigmund, 137

Gallo, Louis, 76n
Game, 7, 12–13, 38–40, 45–46, 52, 61,
64, 88
García Márquez, Gabriel, 124, 126
Genre theory, 7–8, 54–58, 63–64, 66–67,
68, 71–85; Bakhtin and Coover,
71–73; detective fiction, 89, 98,
122–24; dialogic novel defined,
75–76; epic elements in the novel,
99–100; film, 114–21, 136–48; Greek
romances, 78–85, 98; "heteroglossia"
and the novel, 97–98, 102; historical

novel, 85–87; Menippean forms,
77–78; monologic novel, 74; origins:
necessity to genres, 73; pornog-
raphy, 117–20; television and
theater, 131–35; travel novel, 79
Gilda, 143
Goldwater, Barry, 50
Goodgold, Ed, 137n
Gordon, Lois, 57n
Green, Geoffrey, 55, 60, 116
Guarini, Giovanni Battista, 73

Halpern, Daniel, 35
Heliodorus, 72
Heraclides, 28
Herodotus, 28
Holquist, Michael, 72n

Iron Claw, 137–38

Jew as archetype, 65–66, 71
Johnson, Lyndon Baines, 42
Joseph (Old Testament), 23–24
Joyce, James, 3, 25n, 74n, 76n, 80

Kennedy, John F., 42, 51, 70
Kermode, Frank, 9, 18
Khrushchev, Nikita, 62
Kristeva, Julia, 72n
Kuhn, Reinhard, 104n

Lean, David, 146
LeClair, Thomas, 60n, 68n
Light vs. darkness, 50–52, 71, 89,
94–97, 99–101, 104–5, 107, 111,
120–21

McCaffrey, Larry, 55n, 60n, 83n, 116n
Machiavelli, Niccolò, 28
McLuhan, Marshall, 102
Mailer, Norman, 85
Manicheism, 71, 99. *See also* Light
vs. darkness
Marx, Karl, 62
Melville, Herman, 67, 102
Miller, Arthur, 70
Milton, John, 86, 104
Metamorphoses, 3, 15–16, 29–33, 81,
88–89, 103, 107–8, 120, 125, 138,
140–43, 143–45, 146–48
Myth, 7–8, 9–34 passim, 17–19, 112;
America's myth of the sexless male,
109–13; formation of, 46–51,
136–37; ritual reification, 50, 101–2,
133–34. *See also* Civil Religion;
Light vs. darkness; Thresholds

150

INDEX

Naming, 4–6, 37, 39–40, 43–44, 46, 52, 58
Narration (self-reflexive), 53–58, 132, 136–37
Narrator. *See* Creator, disappearance of
Nixon, Richard Milhous, 49, 59–113 passim; *Six Crises*, 79, 82n, 86
Nizer, Louis, 59n
Noah (scriptural), 20–22
Noonday devil, 10–11, 103–4
Novel. *See* Genre theory
Numerology, 5–6, 18, 34, 36, 41, 44–45, 52, 62, 64, 71, 88n, 106

Ovid, 81

Pardo, Don, 126
Payne, John, 73n
Perils of Pauline, 137
Petronius, 81
Phantom of the Opera, The, 138, 140, 141
Pinocchio, 16, 107–9
Play. *See* Game
Plutarch, 28

Rabelais, François, 73–74, 75, 97, 108
Robert, Marthe, 9, 19
Roche, Denis, 57
Roeg, Nicholas, 121, 128
Rosenberg, Ethel, 26, 59

Rosenberg, Julius, 26, 59
Rousseau, Jean Jacques, 70
Ruth, George Herman (Babe), 42

Scholes, Robert, 7–8
Scripture, 19–25, 38, 40–42, 44, 50, 51, 52, 71, 141–42
Shakespeare, William, 15, 38, 115
Singleton, Charles S., 73n
Sophocles, 135
Spenser, Edmund, 116
Sports, 35–36
Stewart, John, 137n

Tanner, Tony, 103n
Taxil, Leo, 25
Thomas, Lowell, 145
Thresholds, 11, 32, 119–20, 124, 125, 133, 137
Todorov, Tzvetan, 89, 114, 115n, 124
Tolstoy, Leo, 74
Tower, Robert, 67n

Valentino, Rudolph, 147
Valéry, Paul, 55

Weiss, Ken, 137n
White, Pearl, 137, 138
Wolff, Geoffrey, 67

Zeno's paradox, 6, 43, 125

Jackson I. Cope is Leo S. Bing Professor of English at the University of Southern California. He is the author of *Joseph Glanvill, Anglican Apologist; The Metaphoric Structure of "Paradise Lost"; The Theater and the Dream: From Metaphor to Form in Renaissance Drama; Joyce's Cities: Archaeologies of the Soul;* and *Dramaturgy of the Daemonic: Studies in Antigeneric Theater from Ruzante to Grimaldi.*

The Johns Hopkins University Press

Robert Coover's Fictions

This book was set in Paladium text and display type by Capitol Communication Systems, Inc., from a design by Ann Walston. It was printed on 50-lb. Sebago Eggshell Cream Offset paper and bound in Holliston Kingston Natural by the Maple Press Company.